The Apple Sauce

A Former Apple Engineer Reveals
Silicon Valley's Secret Sauce to Innovation

Paul A. Martinez

Published by Franklin Publishers
Printed in the United States of America

For permissions, inquiries, or additional copies, contact:
Franklin Publishers
www.franklinpublishers.com

To all you innovators out there…

Who struggle to fit in. Not because you lack value, but because you see value where others don't.

Who live outside of convention, not out of rebellion, but to observe both the boundaries of the present and the horizons of the future.

Who see patterns where others see chaos, opportunity in the overlooked, and beauty in the imperfect, and ask "why not?" where most accept "just because."

Who struggle to balance themselves on that razor edge between genius and madness, obsession and devotion.

Who wake at odd hours, not from restlessness, but from the weight of ideas that won't let you go.

Who bear the scars of rejection, misunderstanding, and indifference, but return again and again, not for praise, but for progress.

Who feel deeply, think relentlessly, and cannot let the world be as it is, because you know it can be otherwise. It will be better.

May the weight of these pressures give momentum to your purpose, shape your vision through their friction, and slow your pace just enough to savor a world you'll forever see as unfinished, yet endlessly becoming.

But most importantly, to my wife Mindy…

Who endures the late nights, the restless questions, the obsessions that will not release me. You live daily with the storm this path creates, and yet you remain my calm. Thank you for loving a man who can never quite put the world down, and for giving me the grace to chase what so often chases me. In doing so, you have given me the one constant I could never invent, your love.

INTRODUCTION

The Sauce, the Stove, and the Signal

Let me be upfront with you: this book is not the deep end of the pool.

It's what's in the ladle.

This is the short, straight-talking version of a much larger work I wrote called *The Infinite Path – The Law of Perpetual Innovation.* That book has many more pages of theories, principles, frameworks, structural foundations, biological evolutionary origins and the economic, thermodynamic and philosophical underpinnings on how innovation really works, what actually drives it, and its implications. And it doesn't just apply to tech companies or product teams, but to all human-driven systems. It's the full theory. The stove, the heat, the ingredients, the mess.

But this one?
This is the sauce.

It's reduced. A bit concentrated.
Tastes like the good stuff because it is the good stuff, just without the density.

And yes, it's flavored by my years as an engineer not only at Apple, but many other companies dating back to Qualcomm in San Diego circa 1996. All through which I learned that innovation isn't driven by creativity, culture, or even technology.

It's driven by tension.
By burden.

By something that doesn't quite feel right and won't stop whispering until someone finally says, "Okay, let's do this. Let's make things better!"

You won't find the usual buzzwords in this book. No "ideation pipelines." No "disruption as a mindset." No "scale-to-unicorn" jargon. What you will find is something real:

- Real friction.
- Real messes.
- Real stories of what actually triggered innovation at one of the world's most admired companies.

And through it all, you'll see a pattern emerge. What I call the Law of Perpetual Innovation (LPI), where:

> Every benefit you create will eventually produce a burden. That burden will demand a new benefit. And the cycle never ends.

You'll see infinity (∞) symbols throughout this book, referencing deeper concepts, principles and laws that live in *The Infinite Path*. You don't need to read it to enjoy this one however, but if something in here sparks your curiosity, that book will take you all the way down the rabbit hole, and then some.

This one is about what matters most:

- Why innovation feels like a fire drill.
- Why most great ideas are actually just good reactions.
- Why every fix comes with a new flaw.
- And why people don't love the features of a product, they love the relief it brings.

This book won't show you how to be a visionary.
It will show you how to be vigilant.

Because the people and companies who win aren't the ones with the most ideas.
They're the ones who are best at noticing tension, responding to it, and staying in the innovation loop, again and again.

So welcome to The Apple Sauce.
Grab a spoon.
And let's get started.

CHAPTER 1
Why Innovation Always Feels Like a Fire Drill

Because Something Broke, Not Because Someone Was Clever

Let's be honest. Most innovation doesn't arrive like a lightning bolt from a brilliant mind sipping cold brew in a conference room. It shows up more like a fire alarm, loud, disruptive, and right when you were getting comfortable.

Despite what motivational posters and TED Talks would have you believe; innovation isn't about vision.

It's about friction.

More precisely, it's about burden. Something isn't working, someone is frustrated, a desire is left unfulfilled, and the status quo is groaning under its own weight. That's when the real work starts.

During my time at Apple, we didn't sit around dreaming about "the next big thing." We were far too busy trying to make the current things frictionless.

If you think a company like Apple runs on perfect ideas, think again. It runs on a never-ending stream of micro-breakdowns, glitches, inconsistencies, dissatisfactions, supply chain delays, user complaints, unrealized user aspirations, and design regrets.

The magic is in how you respond to those burdens and tensions. That's where innovation actually begins.

And it's not glamorous.

Imagine a group of engineers frantically trying to figure out why the latest firmware is sludging half the devices in field testing. Or a designer losing sleep because a color shift on the screen looks different under retail lighting. These aren't "moonshot moments." These are pressure cookers. They don't inspire; they demand.

That's why innovation feels like a fire drill.
Because most of the time, it is.

Not an Idea Problem. A Burden Problem.

There's a myth in the business world that innovation comes from brainstorming. Whiteboards filled with arrows, sticky notes, and slogans like "fail fast."

Okay, there are whiteboards.
But the truth is, most of that stuff never leaves the room.
It dies in email threads and gets buried under PowerPoint decks.

The best innovations, the ones that actually ship and stick, are born out of real-world problems that create just enough discomfort to spark urgent action.

Think about the last time you had a "great idea."

Odds are, it wasn't floating in a vacuum. It probably started with an annoyance.
An unmet expectation.

Maybe a workflow that took too long.
A process that made no sense.
A product that didn't deliver what it promised.

That's not inspiration, it's irritation. An underlying tension between how things are, and how they could or should be.

And it's the single greatest creative force on the planet.

At Apple, some of our biggest leaps came not from dreaming big but from fixing something that might seem absurd to most. That's not to say Apple isn't visionary. It most definitely is.

But vision wasn't what triggered the work.

It was the burden that got our attention.

Even those that go under the radar, that everyone has just accepted as "just the way things are."

That's the first big truth of innovation:

Innovation is not a spark of genius. It's a response to a burden.

Burdens Come First. Always. (∞ - CH 2, CH 22)

That truth is baked into what I call the *Law of Perpetual Innovation* (LPI). A framework I lay out in more detail in *The Infinite Path*.

The short version?

Every benefit we enjoy (we'll call that utility) eventually creates its own new burdens (what I refer to as byproduct in that other book).

Those burdens demand new solutions.
Those solutions create new benefits.
Which, you guessed it, eventually create more burdens.
And the cycle continues.

Remember those prehistoric mobile phones with tiny mechanical keyboards? Each key the size of a fingernail, click-clacking your way through a text like you were sending Morse code from 1942.

It worked.
But it was friction wearing a suit of normalcy.

Touchscreens didn't arrive because someone wanted to be clever. They arrived because thumbs got tired, screens felt too small, and people wanted more without carrying more.

That's the move.

Burden to benefit.

But then?

The new burden surfaced on those early touchscreens.

Sensitivity wasn't good enough.
The glass cracked too easily.
Fingerprints ruined clarity.

You solved one tension and introduced three more.
That's the loop.

Benefit becomes byproduct.
Relief becomes frustration.
The cycle continues.

That's not failure. That's The Law of Perpetual Innovation (LPI).
The system is not broken. The system IS the loop.

This is what The LPI refers to as:
The Byproduct Utility Causality Loop
a.k.a. The Perpetual Cycle of Innovation.

You can't outsmart it.
You can only work with it.

Apple's secret sauce wasn't some vault of ideas.
It was our ability to sense burden early, react quickly, and turn friction into opportunity.

They don't chase novelty, they chase relief.
That's the magic.

So, when you see a shiny new feature or a slick redesign, don't assume someone had a eureka moment. Assume someone somewhere was annoyed or burdened by the status quo.

How Headaches Create Momentum

In engineering meetings, the most valuable person is rarely the most imaginative. It's the person who's the most annoyed, because they're the ones who notice what's not working, and thus see a better potential future.

Innovation loves dissatisfaction.
It feeds on tension.

That's why comfort zones are graveyards for creativity.

We had a guy on my team who used to say, "If it ain't broke, it hasn't been looked at hard enough." And while that might sound cynical, it's the perfect summary of how we approached our work.

Everything was on the table.
Everything was fair game for improvement.
Because we knew that every current benefit had a hidden burden waiting to surface.

Here's a simple rule:

Wherever someone feels pain, friction, or fatigue, innovation is knocking.

The trick is to stop ignoring it.

The Complainer is Your Best Friend (∞ - Principle of Latent Byproducts and Principle of Byproduct Normalization, CH 13. Principle of Utility Integration, CH 16. Innovation Through Utility Integration, CH 24)

We love to roll our eyes at complainers.
But they're often the most honest people in the room.

When customers vent, or employees grumble, they're not being difficult, they're flagging tension the system hasn't addressed yet. Sure, some of it is noise. But often, buried inside that noise is a perfectly accurate diagnosis.

Follow the pain, and you'll find the map.

Take the smartphone.

Before it existed, people were juggling an awkward parade of devices:

- A phone to make calls.
- An MP3 player for music.
- A digital camera for photos.
- A laptop or desktop to surf the web.

If you wanted to stay connected, entertained, and mobile, you had to piece it together yourself.

You had to carry them, charge them, sync them, store them, remember which pocket or bag or room each one was in.

It wasn't a crisis.

But it was friction.
And friction is fuel.
It was normal. But that doesn't mean it was okay.

These were latent and normalized burdens that we had become accustomed to and that laid buried beneath the surface.

Widespread but tolerated.

Until someone finally said, "Why are we still doing it this way?"

And when those pain points got combined, when the music, the phone, the web, the camera all collapsed into one seamless device, people didn't just feel delight.

They felt relieved, and that's what made the delight so real.

The joy came from the tension that was finally gone.
That's innovation.

Not because it's clever. But because it removes what people were silently tolerating.

But don't get too comfortable. Relief never lasts forever. Once the new benefit lands, the new complaints begin: the battery's too weak, the photo quality sucks, the screen's too small, the bandwidth is trash.

This is the loop.

Solve one burden and wait for the next to announce itself.
Because innovation isn't about technology.
It's about tension, specifically, the release of it.

And if you want to find your next breakthrough?

Listen to the people who sound the most frustrated.
They're probably already holding the answer.

Vision is Overrated

People love talking about vision.

Founders give keynotes about it.
Executives make slides about it.
But vision is only useful if it's solving a real burden.
Otherwise, it's fantasy.

There's a famous Steve Jobs quote:

> "You've got to start with the customer experience
> and work backwards to the technology."

It's often misinterpreted as "build something delightful."

But what he really meant was: start with where the friction is in someone's experience.
Then remove it.
That's how innovation lands.

The customer experience isn't some dreamy ideal.

It's a messy, frustrating series of steps people tolerate to get a benefit. The fewer steps, and the fewer headaches you can offer, the more valuable your product becomes.

So don't start with vision. Start with the mess.

Fire Drills Aren't Failures. They're Fertile Ground.

When systems break, teams panic.

But within that panic is a surge of insight. People suddenly become more observant, more collaborative, more creative because there's urgency.

That urgency is uncomfortable, yes.
But it's also clarifying and insightful.

I've been in those late-night sessions where something broke and the whole team rallied. And sure, we were stressed and tired. But those moments created some of the best outcomes we ever shipped.

It's not because we were clever.
It's because we were cornered and committed.

Here's the paradox:

The conditions that make innovation possible are often the ones we try hardest to avoid.

But avoiding discomfort kills innovation.

That's why companies stagnate.
That's why teams lose momentum.

They optimize for smoothness instead of substance. The trick isn't to create chaos. It's to stay attuned to tension so you can respond before the fire alarm goes off.

From Burden to Benefit (Then Back Again)

Innovation is a loop.

First there's a burden.
Then someone solves it.
That creates a new benefit.
That benefit gets adopted.

Over time, from the benefit, new burdens emerge.
Then those get solved.
And on and on it goes.

It's not linear. It's perpetual.
That's why you can't "finish" innovation.
You can only participate in the cycle.

At Apple, we never assumed we had the final answer. We assumed we were in a temporary sweet spot that would soon expire. That mindset kept us sharp. And it made us grateful for tension, not afraid of it.

So the next time something goes wrong, don't panic.

Lean in.
Listen closely.
The burden you're facing is just a prompt.
Innovation is knocking.

Will you be bold enough to answer?

∞ Reference: The Infinite Path

CHAPTER 2

The Problem with Solving Problems

Fix One Thing, Break Three Others

You've probably had this experience: you fix something, anything, and suddenly, two new problems pop up.

Maybe you rearranged your workspace to make it more efficient, only to realize the lighting is now awful and your back hurts.

Maybe your team redesigned a product to make it easier to use, but that tweak caused shipping delays and confused existing users.

Welcome to the most underappreciated law in the world of innovation:

> Every solution creates new friction.

This isn't a glitch in the system. This is the system.

Every time we solve a problem, we create a ripple.
That ripple can be small, like a minor inconvenience, or it can be a tidal wave. But it always shows up somewhere.

At Apple, many of us knew this well. We never launched a new product assuming we had reached "the end."
There was no finish line.

We assumed every fix would reveal new flaws.
That mindset wasn't cynical. It was liberating.

Because when you stop chasing the fantasy of a perfect product, you can focus on what really matters: managing the cycle.

The Byproduct-Utility Cycle (∞ - CH 2)

In The Infinite Path, I introduce something called the Byproduct Utility Causality Loop. Here's the simple version:

1. You notice a burden (an expectation is not being met, or a desire remains unfulfilled).
2. You create a solution (something that provides benefit because it resolved burden).
3. That solution is adopted.
4. Over time, the solution creates new burdens (byproducts).
5. Repeat.

You'll notice there's no "end" to this loop.
That's because there isn't one.
This is innovation's dirty little secret: solving problems doesn't eliminate tension, it just shifts it.

You trade one set of headaches for another. Hopefully, the new ones are better, smaller, or more manageable. But they're still headaches.

Let's make it tangible and more apparent.

When the Fix Becomes the Friction (∞ - Principle of Perpetual Innovation through Byproduct, CH 13)

Apple has spent years making the iPhone thinner.
And thinner.
And then thinner still.

A bulky phone feels awkward in your pocket, hogs space in your bag, and let's be honest, makes you look like you're carrying a fossil.

So, thinner feels better.
Cleaner.
Sleeker.
More modern.

But here's the tradeoff: when you shrink the body, you shrink the room for everything inside. And since you can't just compress internal components in one direction without stretching them in another, you start making compromises.

That's when things get interesting.

The internal circuit board now ends up closer to the backside of the screen. Components that were once isolated start influencing things they were never meant to, like the touchscreen functionality.

For example, some components may start interacting with the touchscreen layer in subtle ways. Not catastrophic, but just enough to introduce squirrely-ness (yes, that's a technical term at Apple). Enough to create weird bugs. Enough to trigger engineering late nights.

So now, a decision meant to improve comfort, usability and aesthetics starts degrading consistency in performance.

Solve one problem. Create the next.

What sets Apple apart, at least in my experience, isn't that they avoid these issues. It's that they go after them. I've seen teams at Apple spend time refining components most companies would consider "not that significant," or "good enough," simply to reduce the small burdens those parts might introduce to the user experience.

Not because customers will ever notice the difference. But because someone within Apple did. And they know that even the tiniest unresolved burden could compound later.

That's the loop. That's the job.

Perfect Products Are an Illusion, But Let's Get Close

(∞ - Principle of Utility as Imperfect, CH 16)

There's a myth that companies like Apple are obsessed with perfection and that every product is some immaculate sculpture of design and engineering.

Let's clear that up: perfection isn't the goal.

But getting as close as humanly possible without breaking the system? That's the game.

Because perfection, in the literal sense, is a trap.

You can chase polish so far that you forget practicality. You can optimize one area so hard that you destabilize three others. You can end up turning something elegant into something unbuildable.

We had a saying back in the day:

"Polish is pointless if the handle breaks off."

Translation? Don't make it beautiful if it's going to snap in someone's hand.

Innovation isn't about flawless artifacts. It's about resilient systems. And resilient systems are built by teams who aim high but stay grounded and resilient themselves. Teams who know how to push right up to the edge of perfection without falling over it.

Because innovation lives in motion. Every tweak is part of a bigger loop. Every improvement shifts something else. Every fix introduces a new constraint.

So no, we didn't chase perfection blindly. But we did chase something better than "good enough."

We chased "excellence with foresight."
Progress with precision.
Relief without regressing.

We weren't building art for a pedestal.
We'd build solutions for the real world.

And when it all clicked and synced. When you've suppressed enough burden, reinforced the system, and made it feel effortless?

It may not have been perfect.
But damn… it sure as hell came close.

The Engineer's Curse (and Blessing) (∞ - Entropy Accumulation, CH 9)

Why are engineers never done?
Because they know too much.

They know every solution they create will decay. They know every fix will age. They know every elegant workaround comes with hidden costs. And this knowledge doesn't make them pessimists, it makes them realists.

Here's something non-engineers don't always understand, good engineers are allergic to the idea of "done." Not because they're control freaks or perfectionists, but because they live inside the loop.

They see the ripple effects in real-time.

They know that the more widely a product is used, the more burdens it creates. Scale magnifies burdens. What worked beautifully for 10 users becomes unbearable for 10 million.

And here's the twist: engineers don't want to be done.

Why? Because being "done" would mean the system is frozen. No more problems. No more challenges. No more learning. And that's not what engineers sign up for.

They're not building monuments. They're building systems that can evolve. And evolution, by its very nature, is messy. That's the whole point.

How the Cycle Powers Growth (∞ - Principle of Byproduct-Driven Utility, CH 13. CH 2, CH 22)

So, if every fix leads to new problems, does that mean we should stop trying? Of course not.

It means we need to upgrade our expectations.
The goal isn't finality, it's flow.

You want to keep moving forward, even if the road swerves a little. You want your system to absorb hits, bounce back, and adjust on the fly, not break.

This is what I call the shift from 'finality thinking' to 'iterative thinking.'

- Finality thinking asks, "How do we get this done right, once and for all?"

- Iterative thinking asks, "How do we get this done right, right now, knowing full well we'll be back here in three months?"

The Byproduct-Utility Cycle isn't a bug in the system.

It is the system.

It's what drives everything forward.

And the better you get at navigating it, the faster your innovation velocity becomes.

The trick is to manage the cost of your burdens.

If a new feature creates friction for 1% of your users, that might be acceptable. If it confuses 30% of them, you've got a problem. Either way, you're going to face new burdens.

The job is to measure, monitor, and adapt.

Beware of the "Clean Sheet" Fantasy (∞ - Principle of Utility Trade-offs, CH 16)

One of the most seductive ideas in innovation is the "clean sheet of paper." It's that moment where someone says, "Let's just start over."

Sounds bold, right?
It's usually a trap.

Starting over means abandoning all the hard-earned insights, feedback loops, and resilience you've built into your current system. It also means that the first 10 problems you solved are going to reappear, often when you least expect them.

At Apple, we rarely threw everything out.

Even major redesigns carried forward lessons and constraints from earlier generations. Why? Because the cycle had already taught us valuable things. And if we ignored those lessons, we'd be stuck solving the same burdens all over again.

You Don't "Fix." You "Trade."
Let me offer you a mindset shift:

> You're not fixing problems. You're trading burdens.

Every improvement is a trade. You reduce one friction and take on another. Sometimes that trade is worth it. Sometimes it's not. But either way, you're not operating in a vacuum. You're in a system and every change affects everything else.

That's why systems thinking is so crucial.

Engineers who succeed aren't just good at solving isolated issues, they're good at predicting where the burden will move to next. They know that the burden doesn't disappear. It migrates, shifts and even changes form.

Think of it like squeezing a balloon. You press on one side, and it bulges somewhere else. Your job isn't to stop the bulge. Your job is to control where it goes, and how big it gets there.

The Best Products Have Known Flaws (∞ - Principle of Byproduct Minimization vs. Elimination, CH 13)

This might sound counterintuitive, but the best products are not the ones with zero issues. They're the ones where the issues are well-understood, well-placed, and non-catastrophic.

At Apple, we launched with known issues all the time. We weren't hiding anything; we were choosing our battles. We asked:

- Where will this friction show up?
- How often will it occur?
- Who will it impact?
- Can we mitigate it?

If the answers pointed to a negligible and tolerable outcome, we shipped. Then we tracked, measured, and iterated. But our prototypes would reach the hundreds of thousands, if not more. So we'd get really close to flawless. At least closer than any other organization I've ever seen on planet earth.

You Are Always Designing for the Next Problem

Here's the ultimate twist: every time you solve a problem, you're actually designing the next one.

Think about that.

When you improve speed, you may increase heat in the product. When you streamline a UI, you may hide important features. When you make something easier, you might make it easier to misuse. Every innovation seeds the next challenge.

That's not failure. That's evolution.

So your job as an innovator isn't to eliminate problems. It's to elevate them. Make the new problems more interesting, more strategic, more worth solving.

That's how progress works.

So what's the Secret?

If you want to innovate like Apple, not copy products but copy thinking, then here's your playbook:

1. Accept the Byproduct-Utility Causality Loop. Don't fight it.
2. Focus on managing burden, not eliminating it.
3. Think in tradeoffs, not fixes.
4. Prioritize real-world friction over abstract ideals.
5. Anticipate where the pain will migrate.
6. Design for the next problem, not the last one.

This is how you stay in the loop without getting overwhelmed by it.

Because once you understand the cycle, you can dance with it.

And that's the secret sauce.

∞ Reference: The Infinite Path

CHAPTER 3

Utility — The Reason People Actually Care

Nobody Wants Features. They Want Relief

Let's talk about the one word that gets thrown around in small innovation circles more than any other: Value.

It shows up in pitch decks, product reviews, investor calls, and UX meetings. But here's the thing, many people using the word have no idea what it actually means.

So let's clear the air. Value means benefit. And socio-economically, this translates to utility.

Utility is just how something helps.

That's it.

It's not the feature list.
It's not the number of settings.
It's not the "technical capabilities."

It's whether or not the product made your life feel a little easier, better, faster, or more enjoyable.

If it didn't? No amount of functionality matters.

And here's the kicker: people don't care about what something can do. They care about what it does for them, when they need it. That's why people don't want features. They want relief.

Relief from confusion. Relief from wasted time. Relief from concern. Relief from friction. Relief from burden.

Utility, Decoded

Let's imagine a hypothetical scenario. You're standing in a room full of product managers, each pitching the next big idea.

- One says, "We've got an AI-based adaptive scheduling engine with predictive inputs."
- Another says, "We made it so your meetings stop overlapping and you can actually go to lunch."

Guess who wins?

The second one.

Because they're not selling features. They're offering relief. And that's what utility is all about, which in turn, translates to value.

The Law of Perpetual Innovation (LPI) defines utility as a response to a burden (byproduct). You don't build things for fun, you build them because something is off, broken, slow, confusing, painful, missing or unfulfilled.

The "thing" that gets built delivers a benefit that alleviates that burden.

But here's where things get tricky:

> The utility you intend to deliver and the utility the user actually experiences are rarely the same.

And that gap is where innovation either wins or dies.

The Gap Between Intent and Experience (∞ - Principle of Intended Utility vs. Experienced Utility, CH 16)

Let me introduce two terms that will change the way you think about product design:

1. Intended Utility: What the designer, engineer, or product manager thinks the product is providing.

2. Experienced Utility: What the user actually gets, emotionally, functionally, contextually.

These two should match. But sometimes they don't.

Why? Because users don't live in spreadsheets. They live in context. They're tired, distracted, frustrated, and juggling real-world constraints. They don't see the beauty in your backend logic. They see whether or not your app crashed while they were in line at Starbucks.

At Apple, we would deeply internalize this reality.

When Utility Adapts Without Asking for Credit (∞ -
Adaptive Utility Innovation, CH 26)

Ever heard someone rave about adaptive antennas?

Probably not. And yet, if you've made a call on an iPhone in the past decade, you've likely benefited from them.

Here's what most people don't realize: inside every iPhone are technologies with names like spatial diversity, MIMO, beamforming, and smart switching.

Sounds like engineering jargon. And it is. But what those systems do is quite elegant: they adapt the phone's radio behavior based on:

- How you're holding it
- Whether you're indoors or out
- Or even whether you're using Wi-Fi or cellular

They exist to:

- Reduce dropped or patchy calls
- Improve data rates
- Extend battery life
- And ensure the device works the way you expect

No matter how you're using it.

Yet, no one asked for adaptive antennas. There were no protests, no surveys demanding spatial diversity and what not.

What there was, however, was a history of frustration and disappointment due to weak signals, short battery life, call drops, inconsistent voice and data.

Those were the burdens.

And while the user never said, "I'll take the iPhone with MIMO beamforming please," the emotional utility came through loud and clear when those burdens quietly vanished.

That's what great innovation does.

It adapts in the background to relieve tension that people may not have even fully articulated.

And Apple didn't just engineer this tech into the phone, they made it mainstream.

They took a behind-the-scenes system and used it to deliver front-line relief.

Because that's the real goal: not features you can brag about, but rather, burdens you don't even realize are gone.

That's utility doing its job. Without needing a round of applause.

Features Are Just Tools. Utility Is the Outcome. (∞ - Principle of Byproduct-Driven Utility, CH 13)

Think of it this way: features are like ingredients.
Utility is the meal.

The presentation. The taste and texture. The exhilaration.

People don't care if your app uses React or Swift (these are programming languages to create apps). They care if an app lets them order dinner from whatever nearby restaurant is still open.

They don't care how many pixels your display has. They care if their aging parent can read the text message without squinting.

They don't care about data compression ratios. They care that their song doesn't skip while jogging.

Utility is how a product feels when it's doing its job right.

And that feeling? It's invisible. It's experienced. And it is always tethered to emotion.

So if you want to innovate, stop asking, "What can we build?" and start asking:

- "Where are people hurting? And in what ways?"
- "What's slowing them down? And why?"
- "What keeps tripping them up?"

"What silent tax are we making people pay, in clicks, confusion, or effort, they never signed up for?"

That's where meaningful utility hides.
Underneath the stuff people wish they didn't have to deal with.

Emotional Utility: The Secret Layer (∞ - Principle of Byproduct Composition, CH 13)

Burden or tension always has two parts to it. The objective part, meaning "the physical thing" that's tripping them up. And the subjective part; "how it leaves them feeling."

At Apple, we understood that relief wasn't just functional, it was emotional.

People don't just want their phones to work. They want them to feel right. They want confidence. Clarity. Delight.

When you tap an icon and it responds with just the right bounce, or when a photo animates into full screen with satisfying smoothness, you're not just witnessing good design. You're feeling good design.

That feeling is utility. It's relief from uncertainty, from clunkiness, from emotional fatigue.

And here's the rub:

You can't fake emotional utility. You can only design for it.

That's why the smallest changes often have the biggest impact.

It's not about adding more. It's about reducing noise, minimizing cognitive load, and clearing the path between intent and action.

Why You Can't Make People Want a Benefit They Don't Feel

This is a painful lesson for innovators.

You can build something amazing. Elegant. Powerful. Efficient. But if people don't feel the benefit, immediately and intuitively, they won't use it.

Utility must be felt, not explained.

Take Samsung.
Over the years, they've packed their smartphones with features that, on paper, sounded impressive: eye-tracking to scroll web pages, air gestures to control the screen without touching it, even heartbeat sensors built into the back of the device.

Novel? Yes.
Intended value? Yes
Useful? That's where things unraveled.

People didn't ask for these features. But that's not what caused them to struggle in the market. The true test came when people didn't feel the relief these features were intending to offer.

Eye-scroll was clunky.
Air gestures worked inconsistently.
The heart rate monitor felt more like a novelty than a necessity.
And eventually, all of them were removed.

These features didn't fail because they lacked sophistication. They failed because they either didn't reduce a burden people actually carried, or they created new ones that people weren't willing to tolerate.

And that's what matters.

When a user can't feel the benefit, they treat it like noise. And eventually, so does the company. Feature by feature, they get removed, not because they were bad ideas, but because they never earned their place in people's lives.

If the user doesn't feel relief, there's no utility.
And if there's no utility, there's no reason to care.

Experienced Utility Is the Only Utility That Matters (∞ - Principle of Utility as Emergent through Interaction, CH 16)

This brings us to a bold but necessary point:

If utility isn't experienced, it doesn't exist.

You can load a product with features, but unless those features translate into clear, immediate, felt benefits, especially in the moments they matter, they are functionally invisible.

Utility isn't defined by what something can do. It's defined by what it can undo. What it removes. That's always the measure.

Not capability.
Not cleverness.
But relief.

Even when that relief is quiet.

Like when your MacBook gives you the option to "Unlock with Apple Watch." It seems small, but it removes the need to type your password every time you lift the lid.

That's not just convenience, it's friction removed.

It reduces interruption, speeds up flow, and gives you back a tiny sliver of energy. Time. Life. Invisible to most. But to someone juggling ten tabs and a train of thought, it's a gift.

That's utility.
That's value.

Not because it adds something but because it removes something that didn't belong.

And yes, this even applies to subtle experiences like peace of mind.

An airbag doesn't go off every day, but you feel safer knowing it's there.

You may never file an insurance claim, but the emotional relief of being covered is very real.

Luxury goods?

Some folks choose luxury watches that are less accurate than the $12 clock in their kitchen.

These items often exist to relieve a social byproduct; the burden of status, belonging, or perceived success. They whisper "You've made it. You're in control. You belong!"

Utility isn't just action. It's assurance. It's confidence. It's the invisible layer that reduces tension without asking for attention.

This is why every design review, every prototype test, and every roadmap decision should focus on one question:

"Where's the relief?"

That question will save you from chasing complexity and keep you anchored to what people actually want and need. Even if they don't know how to say it.

A Quick Utility Test

Here's a simple test I recommend for any product or service. Ask yourself:

1. What burden are we intending to reduce or eliminate?
2. What benefit are they actually experiencing?
3. How quickly will that benefit be felt?
4. What friction might this benefit create?
5. How will we know if people are actually experiencing the relief?

And remember, relief isn't always loud.

Sometimes it's quiet confidence.
Sometimes it's knowing a system won't fail.
Sometimes it's just the feeling that you belong.

If you can't answer those five, stop building.

Because what you're making might be a feature, but it likely won't land as utility.

The Infinite Loop: Utility Breeds Burden Breeds Utility

Let's tie this back to the Law of Perpetual Innovation (LPI).

Here's how it works:

- A user feels a burden.
- You deliver a solution that provides utility (relief from that burden).
- That solution creates new usage patterns, expectations, and interactions.
- Over time, those become the new burdens.

- So you create new utility to relieve those.

And round and round we go.

This is what makes innovation perpetual. Because utility is never final. It's dynamic. It's contextual. And it's always setting the stage for residual burden effects to emerge from it. Because of it.

Which means your work is never done.

So, What Do You Do with This?

You get better at listening.
You prioritize felt benefit over technical specs.
You don't chase features, you chase relief.

You treat utility not as a checklist but as a relationship. A dance between what you built and how the user feels while using it.

And when you get that right? You win.
Not just in sales or retention or brand love.

You win because your product becomes invisible.

It melts and disappears into the user's life. Not because it lacks power, but because it delivered its relief so gracefully, they forgot there ever was a problem in the first place.

That's the highest form of innovation.
That's utility realized, which translates to value delivered.

∞ Reference: The Infinite Path

CHAPTER 4

When the Fix Becomes the Friction

Solving the Old Problem Becomes the New One

Here's a truth that few innovators are willing to accept:

Today's solution is tomorrow's frustration.

It doesn't matter how good it is. It doesn't matter how well it worked. Over time, even the best fix, the best benefit, the best relief, the best utility will eventually start to wear thin. Sometimes literally, sometimes figuratively. This is the heartbreak of innovation:

The fix becomes the friction.

Why Most Innovations Age Badly (∞ - CH 15)

Let's say you launch a sleek new feature, product, or service. It solves a glaring issue. The reviews are glowing. People love it. Your team celebrates.

Fast forward 18 months.

That same beloved solution is now the thing people are complaining about. It feels clunky. It doesn't scale. It introduces new problems. What was once a breakthrough is now the bottleneck.

Why does this happen?
Because innovation doesn't age like wine. It ages like milk.

Innovation thrives in a specific context. It fits a particular user need, a moment in time, a certain ecosystem. But the second the surrounding context changes such as user expectations, tech environments, socio-cultural norms, you name it: that same innovation starts to feel... dated.

This is where the Theory of Constant Utility from *The Infinite Path* comes into play. The theory explains that utility doesn't disappear, but rather its perceived value is constantly under threat from accumulating burdens (byproducts).

Your products utility didn't necessarily get worse. Burdens accumulated over it.

That's the key insight:

Utility doesn't fade because it failed. It fades because it was left behind.

The Invisibility of the Last Win

Here's the curse of being good at innovation: people forget your last success.

You save the customer ten steps? Great. Now those ten steps are gone, and no one remembers them. The relief fades into the background. A new baseline is formed.

And what comes next?
New complaints.

This doesn't mean you did a bad job. It means you did such a good job that the problem no longer registers, and now people are noticing the next burden in line.

This is what some call the gratitude half-life of innovation. It can be short. Extremely short.

Users don't keep score. They keep experiencing. And as long as they're experiencing friction, they don't care what you fixed last year.

That's why innovation is a treadmill.
If you stop moving forward, you get thrown off the back.

So let's take a step back and glance into the rabbit hole of how burdens affect the benefits we so enjoy. Because the reality is:

Burdens that accumulate across our utility end up constraining, overshadowing, even extinguishing the very benefits that once delighted us.

A Doughnut and an iPhone Enter a Bar (∞ - Principle of Byproduct Composition, CH 13. CH 14)

Let's look at how Consumables and Durables both get buried by byproducts.

In classical economics, utility is defined by the type of good you're dealing with.

- The doughnut is a consumable, its utility is delivered in short, sugary bursts.
- The iPhone is a durable, its utility is spread across time, woven into your habits and your routines. Your life.

But under the Law of Perpetual Innovation (LPI), both goods obey the same hidden rule:

Utility doesn't fade because it's weak. It fades because it gets buried.

Let's break that down.

The Doughnut — Fast Utility, Faster Accumulation

It's indulgent, warm, maybe even nostalgic, you close your eyes with the first bite and enjoy away.
But by the second doughnut, the magic is wearing thin.

By the fifth? You're having a one-person identity crisis.

Classical economists call this diminishing marginal utility. The Law of Perpetual Innovation (LPI) calls it byproduct burden accumulation.

And as we stated earlier, byproduct burdens have two parts, the objective reality part of it and the subjective human emotional reaction.

As we eat more doughnuts, the **objective byproducts** can be:

- Our stomach getting full, which equates to physiological saturation.
- Our digestion begins to slow because we're processing more food.
- Our fingers may get greasy and sticky (unless you're into that, until your phone rings and there isn't a napkin in sight).
- There may be a blood sugar spike, bloating, sluggishness, crumbs and messiness.

Yet, as we consume more and more doughnut, the **subjective byproducts**, or human reactions may be:

- Taste fatigue, where the first few bites were exciting, but now feel repetitive.
- Maybe there's regret, and we tell ourselves, "That wasn't worth it."
- Maybe we were cheating on our diet and the guilt says, "I shouldn't have."
- Maybe we get self-conscious, because "Everyone saw me crush five…"
- Maybe we feel a loss of control and agency, "Why can't I just stop?"

The doughnut gives you a spike of joy, then, byproduct burdens begin subtracting from it.

Not because it's broken, but because it's short-lived by design. An extremely compressed utility-byproduct cycle.

The iPhone — Long Utility, Quiet Accumulation

If we look at a durable, like our iPhone, the process is similar.

You don't consume an iPhone.
You live through it.

It wakes you up, guides your calendar, maps your route, lets you pay for dinner, FaceTime your kids, track your sleep. It's invisible until it's essential, and that's what makes its reduction in benefit harder to spot.

Traditional economics would say that its utility is slowly declining.

LPI says that its utility benefit is getting masked and buried under accumulating byproduct burdens.

The **objective byproduct** burdens?

- Battery degradation after 400+ charge cycles.
- OS updates equal app incompatibilities and user interface disruptions.
- Dust in the charging port equals unreliable connection.
- Cracked screen, sticky buttons, dings and scratches.

The **subjective byproduct** burdens?

- Repetitive swipes equal interaction fatigue maybe even boredom.
- "Where did that setting go?" Equals update confusion.
- "Why is my phone suddenly dying at 2 p.m.?" Equals reliability anxiety.
- Feeling obsolete every September equals social pressure to upgrade. (By design? Who knows.)

The iPhone doesn't start to break. It just starts to feel heavier. Not in your hand, but in your mind.

Every second of lag, every mis-tap, every unresponsive swipe becomes a tax. And eventually, the perceived available utility feels less, not because the phone got worse, but because the burdens felt louder.

An example that this is the case.

Go to a third world country. They tend hold on to their iPhones a lot longer. Regardless of scratches, dings, cracks and newer models released. They tend to remove accumulated burdens through repairs.

Why?

Cost is a definite factor, but if we go deeper, these individuals possess a higher tolerance to subjective burdens. Contextually, these individuals are not as intolerant as those in the U.S., where expectations are shaped by marketing, social status and culture.

Under the lens of The Law of Perpetual Innovation, Utility doesn't lose its voice, it gets drowned out.

Utility isn't lost. It's buried.
Everything ages, not through failure, but through burden.

This is what LPI exposes that classical economics doesn't: Utility is never static. It's under constant threat.

The doughnut teaches us that even a tasty joy has a cost, fast and sharp.

The iPhone teaches us that even perfect design can lose its shine, slowly and silently.

In both, it's inevitable.

What matters isn't how useful something was.
What matters is how much burden it ends up accumulating and has to carry now.

The companies that win long-term already know this.
This is why certain companies, especially in Silicon Valley, stay relevant.

They don't treat products as finished, they treat them as temporal carriers of utility, constantly under siege by entropy's disorder, context shifts, and rising expectations.

They design for:
- Decay they haven't seen yet
- Burden the user can't yet articulate
- Relief that feels fresh even when the hardware doesn't

They're not just shipping features.
They're managing the rate of perceived decline.
That's the difference.

Because at the end of the day, you're not just building products. You're managing the rate at which utility gets buried under burden.

And the companies who understand that?

They're not just the ones still standing, they're out there killing it!

Burden Always Finds a Way

It's almost poetic. No matter how perfectly you design something, burden is relentless. It seeps in through the edges, rides along new use cases, gets introduced by scaling, creeps in through shifting norms.

Some of us at Apple, would say, "Out the door and into the fire."

Not in the dramatic, headline-making way. In the quiet ways.
- A menu that at first felt fast may eventually feel slow.
- A button that made sense now seems misplaced.
- A feature that helped now distracts.

And sometimes, it's not the product itself, it's the user. They've changed. Their expectations, habits, and reference points have moved. And your product, as good as it was, is now out of sync.

Burden doesn't need permission. It just shows up.

That's why innovation is not a one-time fix. It's a recurring relationship with tension.

Net Perceived Utility (∞ - CH 9, CH 15)

To quantify what's happening here, The Infinite Path presents the concept of Net Perceived Utility, and the equation is simple:

The utility benefit you perceive to get at any moment in time, is equal to the core utility that a solution provides, minus the total byproduct burdens that have accumulated up to that point in time.

$$U_{Perceived}(t) = U_0 - B(t)$$

- U_0 is the core utility your solution provides.
- $B(t)$ is the total accumulated byproduct (burden) over time.
- $U_{Perceived}(t)$ is the net benefit of what the user actually feels.

This is why even good products feel worse over time. The burden accumulates, subtracting away from the benefit that the user can actually experience. Not always dramatically. Often slowly, subtly, and invisibly.

It's like rust on a car. You don't notice it at first. But then one day, the door doesn't close quite right.

So what's the takeaway?

> Your product is always in a quiet war with entropy's decay.

And if you're not actively managing burden, it's managing you.

Why Updates Feel Like Downgrades

Ever update an App or OS and thought, "Wait… this is worse"?

That's because the fix became the friction. An update, meant to solve an issue or add a benefit, created a new byproduct:

- A setting got buried.
- A button got moved, or worse, removed.
- A visual hierarchy changed.

Even if the overall product improved, the immediate emotional experience worsened.

This is why user testing isn't just about function. It's about perception. It's about emotional continuity. It's about making sure that the relief you intended is actually the relief that's felt.

Legacy Friction: The Ghosts of Past Fixes (∞ - Principle of Open-Ended Byproducts, CH 13)

Here's something we don't talk about enough: legacy friction.

That's when old solutions, patched over, buried under new ones, start causing issues, but no one remembers why they're even there. They become persistent ghosts in the system.

At Apple, we spent enormous time chasing these ghosts. Why? Because the friction they caused wasn't obvious. It was subtle:

- Ways to make the battery last longer for users
- Squirrelly but subtle buzzing emanating from the phone
- Touchscreen accuracy across a huge population of users that all touch differently

It's easy to say, "let's just clean it up." But when those fixes are deeply embedded in live systems, resolving them can cause even more damage.

So, what do you do?

You treat every fix as a temporary scaffold, not a monument. You document assumptions. You create escape routes. You plan for reevaluation.

Because every fix will outlive its usefulness.

Innovation equals Graceful Degradation plus Constant Renewal

Want to build products that age well?
Then build for graceful degradation.

Assume things will eventually go south. Assume systems will shift. Assume your solution will become someone's future frustration.

But also design the ability to renew. To refresh. To swap out. To reroute. To allow for adaptiveness.

This is how you make innovation sustainable. Not by trying to be perfect, but by making your fixes evolve.

So, What Can You Do?

Here's your new playbook:

1. Celebrate fixes but don't worship them.
2. Track burden accumulation over time. Ask what's getting slower, harder, more annoying.
3. Don't assume the user remembers your last win. They're dealing with this week's pain.
4. Treat each fix as a hypothesis. Validate it, monitor it, and prepare to revise it.
5. Design for decay. Assume every fix will fade. Build mechanisms for graceful transitions.
6. Keep tabs on Net Perceived Utility. Use it to balance the benefit you're providing with the friction you're generating.

The Illusion of the Final Fix

The most dangerous phrase in innovation is: "We finally fixed it."

You didn't.
You moved the problem.
You changed its shape.
You kicked the can.

And that's okay, as long as you're honest about it.

Because the real goal of innovation isn't to end friction.
It's to keep moving forward despite it.

That means treating every fix as a waypoint.
Not a destination.

When you can accept that, you'll stop chasing the illusion of the perfect solution and start building products that breathe, evolve, and flex.

And when today's fix becomes tomorrow's friction?

You won't be surprised.
You'll be ready.

∞ Reference: The Infinite Path

CHAPTER 5

You Can't Design Your Way Out of Entropy

Why Simplicity Breaks, Complexity Hides, and Nothing Lasts Forever. (∞ - CH 9)

Let's get something out of the way early

Entropy always wins.

If you've ever wondered why your sleek system starts to feel clunky, your once-efficient process now takes twice as long, or why the elegant solution from last year is today's disaster.

Welcome to entropy.

This isn't just a physics concept about how energy and matter in the universe naturally disperse and spread out over time, moving toward states of greater disorder and equilibrium.

In the world of human-driven innovation, entropy is the natural tendency of any system, whether it's a product, service or process, to fall apart, get messier, or become less useful over time.

And no matter how great your design is, you can't design your way out of it.

Entropy is like Thanos from *Avengers: Endgame*

"...inevitable."

The Innovation Illusion: "If We Just Get the Design Right…"

We all fall for it. The belief that there's a clean, perfect, optimal version of the product or process that, once achieved, will finally stabilize everything.

But here's the law of the universe (and product development):

Everything decays.

- A User Interface (UI) get cluttered.
- Dependencies pile up.
- Documentation becomes outdated.
- Teams forget why certain design choices were made.
- Previously met expectations now fall short.

And even if none of that happens, the context changes.
The user changes.
The technology changes.
The environment changes.
What was perfect in 2023 is a liability by 2025.

This is entropy in action.
And it's not a failure. It's just reality.

Fortunately, all living things fight entropy. That's what makes them alive. They don't just drift into disorder; they spend every ounce of energy holding the line.

Cells repair. DNA replicates. Organisms adapt, conserve, regenerate and reproduce.

But humans? We take it to a whole other level.

We don't just resist entropy biologically; we organize against it.
We write the playbooks.
We assemble the teams.
We build systems to make sure entropy doesn't get the last word, today.

Other species adapt to the storm.
We build shelters, name the clouds, and plan and strategize for the next one.

This is what separates instinctual survival from intentional durability. It's not instinct. It's entropy management with intent.

It's innovation.

And it's how you get ahead of the slow decay before it becomes disaster.

Simplicity Breaks, Complexity Hides

We often praise simplicity. And for good reason, it's easier to use, easier to communicate, easier to sell. But simplicity has a dark side:

Simple things break in obvious ways. Complex things break in hidden ways.

A simple system has fewer places to hide its weaknesses. When it fails, you know exactly where it hurts. That's helpful, but it can also feel dramatic.

A complex system can mask failure for longer. But when it breaks, it breaks hard.

At Apple, we spent enormous effort trying to make extremely complex systems feel simple to users. But under the hood? Absolute madness. Dozens of systems talking to each other, each with its own assumptions, edge cases, and failure points. It worked because we didn't pretend entropy wasn't happening, we prepared for it.

We designed systems knowing they would degrade.

Which brings us to the truth about innovation:

Innovation Is Mostly Fancy Housekeeping

Forget the Hollywood version of innovation; the lone genius, the eureka moment, the press release.

Real innovation? It's much closer to housekeeping.

- Noticing what's out of place.
- Cleaning up messes before they spread.
- Replacing broken things.
- Rearranging workflows.
- Fixing what frayed while no one was looking.

And like all housekeeping, it never ends.

At Apple, this reality took physical form inside rooms, literal rooms, booked with the same reverence you'd reserve for surgery.

Design reviews.
Build readiness meetings.
Failure analysis huddles.
Debugging sessions that pulled in dozens of people across functions and continents.

You'd see whiteboards riddled with issues, spec sheets taped to walls, cross-functional teams pointing at performance anomalies like detectives chasing a suspect across jurisdictions.

The goal wasn't polish. The goal was entropy detection.

Was it a printed circuit board issue? A firmware race condition? A vendor interpretation of a spec that was technically "within range" but practically a disaster?

We didn't wait for failure to become obvious. We hunted for it in the margins.

These weren't innovation meetings.
They were entropy interventions.

And they were some of the most important work we did.

The Real Reason Apple Is So "Innovative"

You want to know the secret?

It's not vision.
It's not magic.
It's not even culture (though that helped a lot).

It's maintenance.

> Apple innovates because Apple cleans up after itself, relentlessly.

Not just with janitorial thoroughness, but with strategic intensity. We expected entropy. We assumed things would fall apart. And we designed teams, systems, and escalation processes to respond to that decay.

That's the real magic: systems and methods that keep themselves from sliding too far downhill.

And when they do slide (which they always do), people are ready.

That's not innovation as a lightning bolt.

It's innovation as a thermostat, constantly adjusting, regulating, and keeping things functional.

Why Nothing Lasts Forever (∞ - CH 12)

It's tempting to believe you can ship something so good, so perfect, so airtight that it won't need updates.

That's a fantasy.

Every product is born into a changing world. What you think is a stable solution today is already degrading by the time your marketing team starts driving the campaign.

- Processes drift.
- Regulations evolve.
- Supply chains get disrupted.
- Users expect more.
- Devices and components age.
- Your best engineers leave.

Even the best design is a temporary state of order fighting against a rising tide of entropy.

So, stop building for permanence.
Start building for recoverability.

Not recovery of the product, but from the invisible byproduct burdens that creep in after the product ships.

The bugs that show up in edge cases.
The shortcuts that stack into workflow clutter.
The quiet friction that slowly rewrites your user's emotional relationship with the product.

That's what recovery means through the lens of entropy: not just getting things working again but returning the user's experience to a place of felt clarity, confidence, and ease.

The Entropy Playbook

Here's what I learned at Apple, and what we practiced:

1. Expect failure – Every process, product, and system will decay. Design recovery points.
2. Detect early – The best way to fight entropy is with early signals. Look for anomalies, delays, confusion.
3. Swarm fast – The longer entropy lingers, the deeper it embeds. Get the right people in the room immediately.
4. Clean as you go – Don't let tech debt or user/customer friction accumulate. Build small sprints to scrub the mess.
5. Archive the why – Decisions decay fastest when no one remembers why they were made. Document your rationale.

6. <u>Test under stress</u> – Entropy accelerates under pressure. Test and simulate edge cases before they find you in the wild.
7. <u>Revisit the basics</u> – The most resilient systems often collapse under basic assumptions. Check those first.

Entropy Isn't Evil. It's the Innovation Engine (∞ - CH 9. CH 11. CH 12)

Chapter 9 of *The Infinite Path* reframes entropy not as the enemy of innovation, but its fuel.

Why?

Because the emergence of byproducts, those burdens, tensions, misalignments, expectations and lingering unfulfilled desires, are symptoms of entropy. They are its embodiment.

And what do byproducts do?
They trigger the demand for new innovation.

So, entropy isn't your opponent.
It's your alert system.
It's opportunity knocking.
It says: "Hey, things are starting to shift. Time to evolve."

This is the deeper truth of the Law of Perpetual Innovation (LPI):

Entropy introduces byproducts. Byproducts demand relief. Relief requires innovation.

So, when your system starts to wobble, don't panic. Listen.

You're being handed your next innovation prompt.

Apple's ~~World~~, no, Universe-Class Reliability Testing

I'll never forget the first time I saw Apple's reliability test labs and capabilities. And I had seen dozens upon dozens of labs in the prior 19 years in industry.

It wasn't just extensive. It was pathologically obsessive.
They didn't just test to standards, they redefined them.

Devices were dropped, twisted, crushed, shocked, charged, drained, baked and so much more. From every imaginable angle. Over and over. And not just a few units; I'll leave that part up to your imagination because that's what it would take for you to believe me.

They simulated realities most users wouldn't even encounter… but might.

And when something failed? Even once?
Engineers would swarm.

Not because the product was broken, but because the possibility of future entropy had just revealed itself.

What Apple had wasn't just a testing process, it was a predictive system for understanding entropy before it showed up in the hands of millions.

I wish I could tell you everything they did.
But out of sheer respect, I won't. Some things deserve to be protected.

What I will say is this:

They didn't just try to build great products.
They tried to build foresight into the physical world.
A crystal ball made out of test jigs, failure logs, and test chambers.

And they succeeded.

Innovation as Order Restoration (∞ - CH 9)

When most people think of innovation, they think of new features, new products, new breakthroughs.

But often, the most valuable innovation isn't about newness.

It's about restoration.
- Making things reliable again.
- Making processes predictable again.
- Making systems coherent again.

But MOST IMORTANT, it's about restoring what the customer experiences. Away from the burdens that have accumulated, back to a place of trust.

Trust that the product won't betray their expectations.
Trust that tapping this button won't cost them their sanity.
Trust that they don't have to second-guess what used to feel obvious.

That's what entropy strips away over time.
And that's what innovation, at its best, restores.

Nothing Lasts. But That's the Point. (∞ - Part 3)

If you've made it this far and feel a little deflated, don't be.
This isn't a story about hopeless decay. It's a call to vigilance.

You can't stop entropy. But you can work with it.

You can design systems that detect it, respond to it, and even anticipate it. You can build teams that treat entropy as a challenge, not a crisis. You can create roadmaps that budget time for renewal, not just release.

And you can build a company that doesn't collapse every time something starts to slide. Because sliding is natural.

The question is: will you catch it in time?
That's the real work.
That's the real win.

And that's what separates temporary success from sustained innovation.

Not brilliance.
Not boldness.

Housekeeping.

∞ Reference: The Infinite Path

CHAPTER 6

The Burdens You Don't See.

Because the Most Powerful Innovation Comes from What People Have Learned to Live With

Most people think innovation starts with a big idea. But most big ideas start with something far less glamorous:

Something people either gave up on, have come to accept or something they haven't even noticed is taxing them.

They're not complaining.
They stopped complaining.
They adapted.
They tolerated.

And that obscurity, acceptance or resignation buried the burden so deeply, even they're not really aware it's there.

This is the invisible frontier of innovation: latent and normalized byproducts.

The burdens people no longer protest.
The headaches they assume are just "how it has to be."
The friction that blends into the background of daily life.

And when you learn to detect those? That's when you stop building incremental features and start building radical shifts.

The Hidden Weight of Normalized Burden (∞ - CH 20.
Exploring Opportunity Across the Byproduct Contrast Continuum - Appendix III)

Most innovations don't fail because they lacked technical genius. They fail because they solved for a burden that didn't matter or missed the burden that did.

But here's the tricky part: some of the most powerful burdens are buried.

They don't show up in surveys. People don't tweet about them. They don't appear in support tickets. These are the burdens people have silently learned to live with.

Like not being able to speak to someone in real time unless they were in the room. Eventually solved by landline phones.

Like having to carry a phone, a music player and a camera. Eventually solved by the smartphone.

People weren't asking for solutions to these burdens back in the day. People simply adapted.

And when people are adapting, the burden doesn't disappear. It just hides.

Until someone digs it up.

Latent Byproduct and Normalized Pain (∞ - Principle of Latent Byproducts and Principle of Byproduct Normalization, CH 13)

In The Infinite Path, this is framed as latent and normalized byproducts.

- A Latent byproduct means the burden is present but not yet consciously felt. They exist without being acknowledged as actual burdens until a superior alternative hits the scene. Once this happens, the gain in efficiency or convenience feels big. Sewing by hand vs. a sewing machine and the relief the latter provided. The whole video rental experience of driving, video availability, rewinding, and returning vs. streaming video. Again, energetic relief.

- A Normalized byproduct means the burden is felt but has been accepted as unavoidable. We build rituals around them, excuses for them, and policies to manage them. We design our day around a limitation we never voted for. Needing to sharpen a pencil was accepted as normal until mechanical pencils arrived. Heating your food in a pan or oven was accepted as the norm until microwave ovens entered our kitchens.

Both of these types of byproducts sap people's energy.
And both are ripe for radical innovation.

Why? Because when you solve them, it feels like magic.

Not because the technology is magical, but because the user didn't even realize how much they needed it until it showed up.

Objective and Subjective: The Two Halves of Every Byproduct (∞ - Principle of Byproduct Composition, CH 13)

As discussed earlier, every byproduct burden has two parts:

1. The objective: measurable, observable or imagined inefficiency. Based on something physically real.
2. The subjective: the emotional-cognitive toll it takes on the user. How their perception of the objective part left them feeling.

The objective side might show up as battery drain, a cracked screen, wasted steps, physical wear, or manual intervention.

The subjective side shows up as expectation deviation or aspirational comparison:

- Expectation deviation is when a product, service, system, even a relationship; anything that is supposed to provide us utility, fails to do what someone thought it would do for them.

- Aspirational comparison is when something works fine but something else shows you what "better" looks like, and your baseline shifts. And now you reframe your once "fine" thing as insufficient.

Even when the objective burden is hidden or minor, the subjective experience is what triggers movement. Because emotion drives Innovation. People leap when the weight of "this could be better" becomes emotionally real to them.

Expectation Deviation: The Promise vs. The Reality (∞ - CH's 11 - 13)

Expectation deviation is when a product or service doesn't live up to what people thought they were getting. And it can happen immediately or over time.

You promised one thing but delivered another. Even small gaps feel like betrayal.

Take the Apple Butterfly Keyboard:

- Objectively, it was an engineering marvel: 40% thinner profile and tighter tolerances. It promised to be compact, and it delivered on that. But thermodynamically, it was vulnerable: dust and debris could jam it up, leading to unresponsive or even stuck keys, creating thermodynamic inefficiency as wasted energy in typing. A tax on the user.

- Subjectively, it created expectation deviation. People expected a keyboard to "just work," and when it didn't, when a single key failed, the "felt" betrayal was disproportionate. The frustration and outrage were less about the key and more about the gap between expectation and experience. That gap was the subjective burden, emergent through distressing emotions. And it was enough to sink the product, even after Apple made fixes to resolve these inefficiencies. But by then, it was too late. The trust was gone.

Aspirational Comparison: The Grass Looks Greener Elsewhere (∞ - CH's 11 - 13)

Aspirational comparison is when users begin measuring your product against something they now know is possible elsewhere. A higher potential utility. It is desire, dressed up as unmet need. It creates tension between what we have now and what we come to believe we should or could have.

Take the iPhone camera's capability, once a user see's what other smartphones are producing:

- Objectively, the byproduct wasn't a flaw in the iPhone, it was that users had now witnessed another device delivering better outcomes. Crisper photos. Cleaner low-light shots. Better portraits. The iPhone hadn't changed, but the bar had. The insufficiency wasn't technical, it was revealed. The iPhone's camera results, once considered excellent, now carried the burden of "not quite enough," simply because something else had made "better" visible. Available.

- Subjectively, the story was aspirational comparison, but the weight was emotional. Once users saw that other phones could capture richer detail, better low-light shots, more cinematic feel, their iPhone, even if still objectively excellent, suddenly felt less impressive. It wasn't just technical envy; it was an emotional reclassification. Their own photos now felt flat. Outdated. Like they were missing out on memories that could've been more vivid. That shift in emotional salience, that subtle disappointment, is the subjective byproduct. The gap between what they have and what they now know is possible.

The burden wasn't that their photos were unusable. The burden was that they had seen better. They had imagined themselves and their memories through a new, more vibrant lens. One they didn't have yet. And in that moment. That gap. Tension emerged.

54

Under LPI, once a higher potential utility benefit becomes real in the eyes of the user, the current outcome or solution inherits the burden of no longer being sufficient.

I'm sure that's what Apple saw. And they responded by bringing multi-lens systems, computational photography, and machine learning pipelines not just to catch up, but to restore the sense of magic users now expected.

You Are Surrounded by Invisible Innovation Prompts
(∞ - Principle of Byproduct as opportunity, CH 13)

If you're waiting for customers to complain, you may already be late. The most powerful innovation cues are:

- The workarounds people stopped or aren't noticing.
- The annoyances people have ritualized.
- The frustrations they've buried under phrases like "it's not a big deal."
- The justifications people use when they say, "It's just the way it is."

This is where the opportunity for radical innovation lives.

Not in the whiteboard session but in the consciously and subconsciously tolerated pains.

The Problem with "Innovation Labs" (∞ - Principle of Utility as Reactive, CH 16)

Many companies build innovation labs. They fill them with designers, strategists, and post-it notes. But here's the problem:

Innovation can't be abstracted. It has to be embedded.

Labs often get disconnected from the real burdens that are actually fueling a business. They can end up floating in a bubble of hypothetical theory and mockups. Meanwhile, the real innovation opportunities are piling up in support queues, complaint logs, or out there in the real world, in the lives of users. Waiting to be unearthed.

If your innovation team isn't exposed to the headaches of your customer base, they're not innovating. They're hypothesizing. They're guessing.

Why Most Teams Miss It

Most teams look for the signal in the noise.
That's perfect for incremental sustained innovation.

But radical innovation often hides in the silence, below the noise floor.

People won't complain about what they think is permanent or normal because everyone around them is experiencing it in the same way.

And that's the moment to lean in.
To investigate what isn't being said.
To poke at the assumption behind "we've always done it this way" or "this is just the way it is."

The Real Work: Unearthing Unspoken Burdens (∞ - Radical Innovation, CH 28)

Want your next product to matter?
Don't just ask what people want.
Ask what they gave up on.
Ask what they quietly accept.

Sense where they're literally burning more calories to extract the benefit; physically, cognitively, emotionally, socially, and contextually.

Because buried inside those abandoned hopes, silent frustrations and invisible energy sappers is where radical demand is quietly waiting.

Innovation doesn't begin with imagination.
It begins with rediscovery.

Rediscovery of needs people once felt but stopped voicing.
Rediscovery of friction they've never questioned.
Rediscovery of tension they no longer resist.

Find that, and you won't need to manufacture demand.
You'll uncover a hidden desire that was there all along.

And when you relieve a burden people didn't know they were carrying?

That's not just innovation.

That's radical innovation.

Be the One Who Notices (∞ - Principle of Innovation Triggering, CH 13)

If there's one skill I'd teach every new hire, every product manager, every designer, every marketer, it's this:

Learn to notice what everyone else tolerates.

Because the thing that people shrug off? That's often the exact thing that's breaking flow, trust, or value.

When you train yourself to see that, you become dangerous in the best way.

You stop waiting for ideas to arrive.
You start spotting where they're already needed.

And then, instead of innovation being some mysterious act of creativity, it becomes what it actually is:

Innovation is a human response to human friction.

Reducing the amount of emotional, cognitive and physical energy that people have to spend. On the frictions and burdens that the current product or system is now forcing upon them:

- Screens that scratched and cracked easily, obstructing our view or annoying us.
- Headphone cables that tore or broke from wear and tear, messing up our experience.
- Texting people misspelled words, then needing to send corrections afterwards.

We innovate by helping people get back their freedom by refocusing those energy costs back on what matters to them:

- Being able to see what's on their screen even after a few drops and tumbles.
- Being able to listen to their music without needing to be tethered to a cable.
- Being able to send correctly spelled text because of autocorrect, or post-sent editing.

∞ Reference: The Infinite Path

CHAPTER 7

Everyone Wants the Sauce. No One Sees the Stove.

Why Outsiders Think It's "Vision," But Insiders Know It's "Vigilance"

Let me let you in on a secret that would've ruined a thousand breathless tech headlines:

Apple's real secret isn't vision. It's vigilance.

Yes, the keynote moments are amazing.
The black turtleneck was great.
The One More Thing.

The slow camera panning across aluminum, steel or titanium curves and beautifully timed swipe gestures.

That's the sauce that the world sees.

But that's not where the magic happens.

The magic is on the stove.

The hard, messy, relentless work that goes on backstage.

The constant, obsessive, borderline neurotic process of noticing what's not yet right, and refusing to let it slide.

Because here's the truth:

The sauce only tastes magical because someone stayed up all night laboring over the stove.

The Illusion of Vision

People assume Apple has some mystical foresight. That they know what the market will want years in advance, and we're just patiently waiting to unveil it.

That's... not how it works.

Yes, there are long-term bets. Yes, there's taste. But most of the breakthroughs happen because someone noticed a burden. A subtle, creeping flaw. And decided not to wait for it to become a disaster.

It's not vision.

It's vigilance.

We didn't have a magic ball.
We had process and pacing.

And a company-wide instinct to hunt down friction before it showed up in the user's hands. Or it had been there all along, and we addressed it.

The Process Is the Product (∞ - Byproduct-Driven Innovation)

Here's what most people don't realize:

Apple's true innovation isn't just their products. It's the system that allows them to be built at all.

That system was built on:

- Cross-functional reviews
- Burden surfacing rituals
- Internal escalation playbooks
- Quality gate and readiness reviews
- Parallel sprint and rework cycles

Every team, from product design to integration to software to supply-chain to retail, had ways of identifying burdens before they metastasized.

This wasn't just troubleshooting. It was a form of organizational reflex.

And once you develop that reflex, it becomes second nature:

- You don't wait for customer complaints.
- You don't rely on test plans to catch everything.
- You build muscle memory around noticing what is off.

That's what we were really doing.
Building a company that could feel the heat before the flame.

The Stove Is Always On

Here's something you learn quickly at Apple:

There's always something burning.

Maybe it's not visible yet. Maybe it's not even measurable yet. But somewhere in the system, a small misalignment is starting to ripple.

Maybe a margin tweak is throwing off a print spec.
Maybe a UX decision is confusing 3% of users in edge cases.
Maybe a firmware update fixed a bug but slowed boot times.
Maybe a very small buzzy sound has been noticed by an Exec.

You don't always know where the smoke is coming from. But you know to listen for the sizzle.

And when you hear it?
You don't wait.
You swarm.

Because what may look like a "tiny" bug might be the start of a multi-million-dollar headache.

The Story of a Ghost We Couldn't Catch

During one Apple Watch program, one of our top engineers, we'll call him Dr. A, found something strange. A weird electrical noise. Just a blip. A hum. Not in the code. Not in the circuit board layout. It came from a standard component: a resistor.

It wasn't repeatable. It wasn't predictable. It didn't even show up in spec sheets. We called it "Dark Noise" because no one could see where it was coming from.

We pulled in suppliers. Ran experiments. Obsessively combed through board variations. Was it dangerous? No. Would a user ever notice it? Likely not, maybe 1 in 10 million.

But it bugged us.

And that's the point.

Because that's what it's like inside the stove: you're haunted by things most people will never see. And eventually, when the trail went cold, we just swapped in a precision resistor and moved on.

We weren't building research papers. We were building a product.

But that ghost still lingers.

Because real innovation isn't about eliminating every unknown, it's about knowing which one's matter, and which ones are worth obsessing over... even if no one's watching.

Why the Sauce Looks Like Magic

To outsiders, it all seems seamless.

The animations.
The unboxing.
The typography.
The packaging that opens with a soft hiss.

It feels effortless.
But that feeling is manufactured.

It's built from thousands of decisions to tackle tiny burdens no one else would've even noticed. It's built from late-night sessions, readiness reviews, user testing, and internal triaging and escalations.

Effortlessness is what it looks like when people do really hard things in the background.

The sauce is real.
But it came from the stove.
And the stove is always on, and there are always thousands laboring and toiling over it.

All so that the sauce feels smooth, sexy, effortless and ultimately, surprising and delightful.

And I think I can speak for almost every engineer, technician and individual contributor…

Thousands of hours of our time in exchange for those few real moments of joy on the user's face.

Worth it. Always. Every single time!

Constant Byproduct Hunting as a Cultural Reflex (∞ - Byproduct-Driven Innovation)

This is what really made Apple different.

Almost everyone, from interns to VPs, had developed the instinct to hunt byproducts.

Does Apple hire for it? I'd say we'd instinctually look for it in a candidate.

Is it infectious? Absolutely.
Did it slow things down? Sometimes.

Did it create more work? Always.
Was it worth it? Without a doubt.

Because once you start thinking in terms of burden, your whole outlook shifts:

- You stop assuming things will work.
- You start wondering how they'll break.
- You stop celebrating features.
- You start protecting the user from friction.

And once that habit takes hold, it scales. It propagates. It becomes culture.

That culture is what enables the innovation, not charisma.
Not genius.
Not luck.

Just relentless burden detection and response.

Why Most Companies Miss It

You know why most companies can't replicate this?
Because they're too focused on output.

They want the product, the press, the promotion, the prestige and the profit.

They haven't internalized that those are the benefits that naturally follow the resolution of deeply human burden.

They invest in storytelling more than cleaning up the mess before it happens, or worse, the mess after it happens.

And when something breaks?

They patch it.
They spin it.
They shrug.

What they don't do is rewind the tape to find the source burden.
The byproduct that was ignored, downplayed, or dismissed.

Apple doesn't win because it's better at ideas.
It wins because it's better at vigilance.
And it keeps winning precisely because it doesn't do what other companies do.

Rely on surface rather than substance.

Byproduct as Opportunity (∞ - Byproduct-Driven Innovation. CH 13)

In *The Infinite Path*, one of the core principles is Byproduct as Opportunity.

Here's the concept:

Every burden, every unintended consequence, every hidden friction or unfulfilled tension is a potential breakthrough in disguise.

Byproducts aren't failures. They're clues.

- A UI tweak triggers confusion? That's a sign you haven't nailed the interaction.
- A firmware update slows boot time? That's a chance to rework efficiency.
- A customer skips your onboarding? That's a prompt to simplify setup.

In every friction is the seed of your next innovation.

But only if you're watching.

Everyone Wants the Sauce. Few Can Handle the Stove.

It's easy to admire the outcome.
The launch.
The polish.
It's harder to admire the kitchen it came from.

Because the kitchen is hot. It's crowded. It's full of dropped ingredients, abandoned processes, and raw problems.

But it's where the magic is made.

And if you want to build something people remember, you can't just want the sauce. You've got to learn to love the stove, with all the heat and messiness.

Otherwise, get the hell out of the kitchen.

So, What Do You Do with This? (∞ - Byproduct-Driven Innovation)

Here's how to build your own version of the stove:

1. Hire Burden Hunters – People with the integrity, resilience, motivation and empathic sense to relentlessly unveil burdens.
2. Build Feedback Loops – Make it easy and safe for people to raise concerns.
3. Create Cross-Functional Triaging – Don't silo problem-solving. Mix disciplines early.
4. Reward Vigilance – Celebrate people who prevent issues, not just those who solve them.
5. Keep a Byproduct Log – Track unintended consequences. Look for patterns.
6. Measure Response Time – How long does it take to swarm an issue? Get faster.
7. Train for Off-ness – Don't just train to execute. Train to notice what's not quite right.
8. Normalize Escalation – Escalation isn't a failure. It's a function. As a leader, never allow your people to accumulate burdens.

If you do that, you'll build a team that doesn't just admire innovation.

You'll build one that creates it, before the world even knows it needs it.

Taste the Sauce, But Don't Forget the Stove

It's fine to love the product.
To geek out on the box.
To admire the curve of the glass.

But just remember:

Everything beautiful you see came from someone catching something ugly early.

Someone listened to a weird complaint.
Someone stayed late to rerun a test.
Someone stopped a build because a seemingly minor dimension was off.

The sauce is what's celebrated.
But the stove is what's responsible.
That's where innovation really lives.

And that's where you should be looking.

∞ Reference: The Infinite Path

Chapter 13 – The 56 Byproduct Principles

See index for Byproduct-Driven Innovation, including AI-BDIE (Artificial Intelligence based Byproduct-Driven Innovation Engine)

Chapter 8

Don't Fall in Love with the Idea. Fall in Love with the Burden. The Tension.

Because Ideas Are Cheap, and Headaches Are Everywhere

Let's get this out of the way:

Ideas are not rare. Sensitivity is.

We live in a world overflowing with ideas. Apps. Products. Interfaces. Features. Business models. AI-powered everything these days. But if you look closely, most of it isn't innovation, it's noise. It's people chasing novelty instead of burden.

I recently wrapped up an AI program through MIT. One stat they shared stuck with me: nearly 80% of enterprise AI deployments fail (2024 RAND Report). And the top reason? "Unclear business objectives."

Let me decode that for you: "We don't know what we're trying to fix, but everyone else is doing AI, so we better jump in too."

I see this firsthand today. Silicon Valley AI vendors show up with sleek platforms in search of a problem to attach themselves to.

It's backwards.
It's like developing the medicine before you even diagnosed the illness.

This is exactly what many businesses, large or small, still do.

They confuse invention with innovation.
They chase brilliance instead of burden.

Or worse, they try to manufacture burdens in the minds of consumers, "If you don't act now, you could lose out!"

And when it fails, they wonder why.

They believe that ideas lead to innovation.
They fall for their solutions instead of the burdens that truly precede them.

They believe it's about creativity instead of sensitivity.

But the problem isn't a lack of imagination.
It's a lack of attunement.

Real innovation doesn't begin when someone has a brilliant idea.
It begins when someone feels that something's just not right and refuses to look away.

Creativity Is Easy. Sensitivity Is Hard. (∞ - CH 21)

Everyone wants to be seen as creative. Everyone wants to be the genius who came up with the game-changing idea. But here's the paradox:

The best innovators aren't the most imaginative. They're the most observant and emotionally attuned.

They're the ones who notice the hesitation in a user's behavior.
They feel the slight friction in a workflow.
They hear the repetition in customers that others tune out.

They empathize with what is communicated through tone, body language and expression.

That's what we valued most at Apple.
Not the person with the flashiest mockup.
But the one who noticed the burden before it became obvious.

Sensitivity is a superpower, not a weakness.

Because when you're tuned to tension, innovation becomes a natural response.
Not a forced act.
Not a grand performance.

Just a quiet leap away from burden.

The Dangerous Seduction of Your Own Genius

The moment you fall in love with your idea, you become blind and deaf to your user's tension.

That's not romantic. That's risky.

Engineers and scientists, we've all done it. Built something we were sure people would love. Bragged about its potential. Pushed it into the world.

And then... silence. Or worse, confusion.
Because we weren't solving. We were performing.

Genius is not what people admire. Relief is.

Einstein is best known for his Theory of Relativity, which unburdened humanity from the old limits of physics by revealing that space, time, gravity, and matter are dynamic, interwoven, and relative.

People don't remember skill, ability or cleverness (Maybe, sometimes). But what matters to them the most is how it affected or impacted them.

They remember the moment something hard became easy for them. Something annoying became enjoyable. Something stressful became comforting. Something difficult became easy.

You can only get there by focusing on their burden, not your brilliance.

From Friction to Insight to Solution

Here's the real innovation sequence:

1. Friction – Something doesn't feel right.
2. Observation – You notice, examine it, and re-examine it.
3. Insight – You uncover the root cause or deeper pattern.
4. Solution – You respond with something that delivers freedom and relief.

If you start at #4 (solution), you skip the most important work.

I have first-hand consulted companies that start at #4 and justify themselves backwards.

That's why so many "innovations" feel disconnected.

They weren't born of friction.
They were born of ambition.
Or ego.
Or mimicry.

The best innovations, the ones that land, stick and spread, follow this sequence because they begin with real-world tension.

At Apple, we didn't ship features because they were flashy.

We shipped them because they addressed something annoying, dissatisfying, tension-relieving and long overdue. And then we polished them until they felt like magic.

But from what I gathered; magic was never the goal. Nor flashiness.

It was always "felt relief." That moment when a user thinks:

"Yesss, thank you!"

That's the moment we built toward.
Because true innovation isn't brilliance, it's benefit.

And that benefit shows up as tension that finally let's go.

Forescension: The Leap Away from Burden (∞ - CH 22)

In *The Infinite Path*, I introduce the concept of Forescension.

It describes the moment when someone becomes emotionally and cognitively ready to leave a familiar, burdensome state and leap toward something better and more promising.

It's not just logic.
It's not just about a list of pros and cons.
It's about emotional salience.

People don't leap because they can.
They leap because they "feel" they must.

Forescension is the ignition point where burden becomes intolerable or where a new possibility becomes so emotionally resonant that the current state can no longer be justified.

It's the tipping point of felt contrast between where I am now, and where I must be.

A user won't abandon a clunky system because you pitch them a shinier one. They'll abandon it when the burden of staying outweighs the fear of changing, and the benefit of changing feels real and undeniable.

That's when innovation lands.

Forescension is not a leap toward novelty, it's a leap away from tension.

A leap away from pain, inertia, waste, invisible emotional drag.

If your idea doesn't connect to a felt burden, small or large, people won't forescend.

They'll stick with what they know, even if it's awful.

That's why your idea must be grounded in a tension or burden, not theory or imagination.
In pain, not potential.

You Don't Need More Ideas. You Need a Better Antenna. (∞ - CH 20)

The most effective innovators aren't idea factories. They're tension sensors.

They know how to:
- Listen for repetition in complaints
- Spot hesitation in user behavior
- Detect confusion in onboarding
- Hear frustration in customer support tickets
- Notice the workaround in someone's process

Each one is a flare. A signal that forescension is possible.

And your job is to show up with a better alternative, one that removes friction so completely, or at least emotionally relevant, that the jump feels obvious.

You don't need fireworks.
You don't need a pitch deck.

You need to hand them the kind of relief that lets them finally put the burden down and not look back.

Falling in Love with Burdens

At one point in my stretch at Apple I was supporting the Watch program, helping deliver component solutions to the System Integrators. These are the engineers responsible for stitching together existing, improved, and brand-new functionality for the next product release.

They didn't need just parts.
They needed parts that made their trade-offs survivable.

- The space they had to work with? Tiny.
- The performance targets? Unforgiving.

- The timeline? Relentless.
- The volumes? Tens of millions.

So I stopped asking, "What do you need?"
And started asking, "What's in your way?"

I didn't just gather specs, I gathered burdens.
I studied their pain points like a safecracker eyeing a vault, because I knew there was something valuable locked inside:

Insight. Clarity. Leverage.

And the more I looked, the more their constraints, trade-offs, and quiet frustrations started to feel personal.

They stopped being theirs and started becoming mine.
That's when everything changed. That's when the real work began.

I won't go into detail of how I removed some of these burdens, but I'll share one of the simplest yet impactful one's.

I'd nickname certain components as shorthand memes, "The Fat Baby," and "The Crawling Baby," to make them easier to remember than part numbers. The names stuck because they were born from shared context, not from a spec sheet.

This served as cognitive burden removal.

And yet, there was another group at Apple whose official job was to deliver these kinds of components. One day, that team's lead pulled my boss and I into a meeting to say, "Hey, just so we're clear, we own this space."

Afterward, my boss laughed and said something I'll never forget: "How do you own capacitors at Apple?"

Here's the truth:
Some people stay removed from the action.
Others step directly into the mess, the late nights, the unspoken workarounds, the friction behind the friction.

I wasn't ever going to feel what the System Integrators felt.
But I decided to treat their burdens as if they were mine to carry.

I internalized them. Got obsessed with them.
I had fallen in love with the burdens.
Not because I had to.

But because solving them became imperative to removing
burden from my internal customer.

That's what it means to innovate from burden.
You get so close to the heat that you stop
guessing.

You stop performing.
And you start relieving.

When to Kill Your Idea (∞ - The Principle of Byproduct-Driven Utility - CH 13, The Principle of Utility as Reactive – CH 16)

Here's a painful but necessary truth:

If your idea isn't grounded in burden, it has to go.

Even if it's beautiful.
Even if it's brilliant.
Even if you've already invested months.

Because without tension, there's no pull.
Without burden, there's no trigger.

People don't adopt because they're impressed. They adopt
because they're relieved.

Kill the idea.
Save the attention for something that actually matters.

And yes, there will be solutions grounded in burden that are
appealing at first glance.

But if they're spawning new burdens or awakening old ones, then you need to focus on what has the most overall effect of "net relief."

Fall in Love with the Right Problem

You've heard this advice: *"Fall in love with the problem, not the solution."* This is a book by Uri Levine, the Co-Founder of WAZE.

It's true. But I'd tweak it a bit:

Fall in love with the emotional strain; the burden, the tension.

The lived and felt burden. The actual pain. The invisible tripwire.

When you fall in love with burden, you become loyal to the user, not to your own cleverness. You stay close to what they need.

This is where many lose sight of the task at hand. Subconsciously prioritizing what they want for the user.

But the job is simple:

We don't build for them. We build from them.

And that's what creates trust.
That's what creates traction.
That's what makes people jump.

The Tension Is the Treasure

The market doesn't need more ideas.
It needs more people who are brave enough to sit in the discomfort and say, "Something here isn't working for my user."

Those are the real innovators.
Not the visionaries.
Not the storytellers.
Not the geniuses.

The ones who feel the burden and make the leap.

That's forescension.
That's the moment of innovation.
That's the work.

So next time you think you have a big idea, stop.

And ask yourself:

Whose tension is this relieving? Mine, or theirs?

If you can answer that honestly, clearly and powerfully, you're on the right path.

If not?
Let it go.
Go back to the true source of the burden.

That's where the treasure is.
That's where the work begins.

∞ Reference: The Infinite Path

CHAPTER 9

What Silicon Valley Still Gets Wrong

Features Over Feelings, and Why That's Backwards
(∞ - CH 16)

If there's one thing I could tell every startup founder, every product manager, every pitch-deck-slinging VC in Silicon Valley, it's this:

> Utility is not your feature list. Utility is how people feel when they use your product.

But that's not what gets prioritized.

In many tech circles, innovation still looks like specs, capabilities, patents, metrics. People fall in love with what their product can do. They optimize for scale, speed, and cost.

And in doing so, they miss the most important thing:

> Relief. Clarity. Confidence. Because that's what people actually buy into.

They don't buy features. They buy the feeling of something working so well, it disappears into their life.

The Spec Sheet Is Not the Product

Let's imagine a real-world example. Two startups launch competing products. Same core functionality. One has more features, more knobs to turn, more settings to play with.

The other has fewer features, but every step is intuitive, responsive, and smooth.

Guess which one wins in the long run?

Not the one with the bigger list of features.

It's the one that delivers the most emotional-cognitive utility. The one that reduces anxiety. The one that doesn't require a user manual. The one that doesn't feel like work.

At Apple, this was religion. We didn't care how much something could do. We cared how much burden it removed.

And that burden? It wasn't just technical. It was psychological.

- Confusion is a burden.
- Overwhelm is a burden.
- Uncertainty is a burden.
- Inconvenience is a burden.

If your product adds any of those, even if it's packed with power, you've lost.

Subjective vs. Objective Byproduct Revisited (∞ -
Principle of Byproduct Composition, CH 13. Capturing Objective Byproduct, CH 19. Harnessing Subjective Byproduct, CH 20)

We've already touched on the two dimensions of byproduct:

- Objective Byproducts: The physical stuff. Slower load times. Excess clicks. Battery drain.
- Subjective Byproducts: The emotional stuff. Frustration. Confusion. Insecurity. Hope. Desire.

It's relevant to emphasize again because:

Many engineers focus on the objective ones. And that's fine. But the subjective byproducts are what actually trigger user abandonment or user loyalty.

Why? Because humans don't think in megabytes and nits. They think in feelings.

A 10ms delay doesn't mean anything until it feels like "something's off."

A misaligned button isn't a bug until it feels like "I don't trust this."

> Subjective byproduct is the emotional residue of an experience that feels off, or a possibility that feels promising.

And some in Silicon Valley largely ignore it, because it's hard to wrangle. And even harder to quantify.

But that's what makes it so powerful.

Because once you tune into it, you'll see opportunities your competitors miss completely.

What I'd Tell Every Startup If They'd Listen (∞ - CH 13, CH 19, CH 20)

If you gave me five minutes on stage in front of a room of founders, here's what I'd say:

1. Stop building features. Start reducing burden.
2. Track how people feel, not just what they do.
3. User delight is not a nice-to-have. It's your differentiator.
4. Every option or feature, if not removing burden, is adding it.
5. Clarity is a feature. Trust is a feature. Flow is a feature.

And I'd finish with this:

> Your product is only as good as the relief it provides.

You can ship five features a month and still lose if the user walks away feeling tired.

Engineering for Byproduct Avoidance (∞ - CH 10)

This might be the biggest mindset shift of all.
Most teams engineer to add what they understand as value.
More features. More capabilities.

At Apple, the pattern I observed that stood out the most was that ~80%+ of engineers were engineering to avoid burden.

Every design decision was essentially filtered through this question:

What burden might this create later?

- Will this interaction confuse?
- Will this setting overwhelm someone?
- Will this feature break flow?
- Will this option become Inconvenient?

I didn't see us as building to serve a roadmap. I saw us as building for resonance.

And resonance comes from one thing:
The removal of unexpected, unwanted friction.

If that's not part of your engineering criteria, you're building a house of burden.

The Myth of the Rational User (∞ - CH 20)

Another thing that some in Silicon Valley get wrong?

They assume users are mostly logical.
We're not. At least not most of the time.

We're human.

Which means:
- We're emotional.
- We're inconsistent.

- We don't read the instructions.
- We tap the wrong thing.
- We get impatient.
- We get frustrated.
- We feel dumb when something doesn't work for us.

And that emotion, the one of feeling inadequate, can be the single biggest churn factor.

No one wants to feel stupid using your product.

So, if your app makes them hesitate, if your interface shames them, if your copy confuses them, you've failed.

Even if the feature works perfectly.

You're Not Designing for Function. You're Designing for Confidence.

Utility isn't just functional. It's primarily emotional coherence.

It's the feeling of:
- "This makes sense."
- "This responds the way I expect."
- "This helps me do what I came here to do."

That's why Apple focused so much on affordances, transitions, gestures, feedback. We weren't just designing an experience. We were designing reassurance.

Every tap, every animation, every sound, was a way of saying, "You're okay. You're on the right path. Keep going."

In my opinion, that's what made people love the product.
Not the specs.
Not the power.
But the feeling of flow.

Feelings Scale. Features Don't.

You can keep adding features. And for a while, it might work.

But eventually, you hit a wall:
- New features create complexity.
- Complexity creates friction.
- Friction creates confusion.
- Confusion creates drop-off.

But feelings? Feelings scale.

If you make someone feel good using your product, they tell people.
- They stay longer.
- They explore more.
- They forgive bugs.
- They stick around.

Because they're not loyal to your feature set.
They're loyal to how you made them feel.

What We Did Differently at Apple

We didn't focus on "ship fast."
We focused on "ship consistently," and everyone knew what September meant.

But most importantly, we shipped things that felt inevitable.

Because we sweated every subjective byproduct:
- "Does this interaction reinforce trust?"
- "Is this moment worth the user's attention?"

We didn't just provide utility. We built confidence loops.

And that's why people stuck with the ecosystem.
Not because they couldn't leave.
But because they didn't want to go back to feeling worse.

If I Could Rewrite some of Silicon Valley's Product Briefs (∞ - Principle of Strategic Byproduct Selection, CH 13)

Typical product briefs ask:
- What problem are we solving?
- What features will address it?
- What metrics will we hit?

Here's how I'd rewrite it:
- What burden does the user currently feel?
- What negative emotion does that burden produce?
- How can we remove that emotion as elegantly as possible?
- What feelings do we want to create in its place?
- How will we know we've succeeded, emotionally, not just functionally and objectively?

That's a product worth building.

Regions of Silicon Valley Don't Need More Tech. They Need More Empathy.

We have enough tools.
We have enough features.
We have enough clever ideas.

What is lacking in some of these companies is emotional attunement.

We need teams who obsess over the emotional state of the user. We need designers who ask, "Will this make someone hesitate?" We need engineers who say, "Let's make this feel natural and intuitive."

Because in the end, your success won't come from being first to market.

Or from raising the biggest round.
Or from shipping the most features.

It will come from this:

You made someone feel better.
You noticed their burden.
You relieved it.
And they remembered.

That's utility.
That's innovation.
That's what some parts of Silicon Valley still don't get.

∞ Reference: The Infinite Path

CHAPTER 10

The Real Secret Sauce

It's Not Tech. It's Tension Detection (∞ - Principle of Strategic Byproduct Selection, CH 13)

People love to ask: "What's Apple's secret sauce?"

Some think it's design. Some say it's supply chain excellence. Others claim it's marketing, or product timing, or the cult of leadership.

But if you've ever worked deep inside the machine, you know:

> The real secret sauce isn't technology. It's masterful tension detection.

That's what Apple does better than anyone else. It notices where things don't look right, don't sound right, don't feel right, often before those things become problems. And they move fast to address them. Most often before they even enter the market.

You won't see knee-jerk fixes.

Instead, you see thoughtful, meaningful, systemic responses that often created entirely new innovations.

That's the sauce.

And it's one any company (with good designers and engineers of course) can make if they're willing to develop the same reflexes.

The Best Innovators Are Burden-Hunters (∞ - CH 10. CH 11. Principle of Innovation Triggering, CH 13)

Forget vision. Forget genius. Forget being "disruptive."

The people who consistently deliver great innovation aren't those dreaming the biggest. They're those noticing the smallest.

Innovation isn't born from inspiration. It's triggered by byproduct. The burdens and tensions that existing utility methods have imposed on us.

We're talking about the engineers who catch a UI inconsistency that may or may not confuse users down the line. But they wrangled that tiny beast.

The packaging manager who realizes a label spec may break under thermal pressure.

The service rep who hears the same customer confusion for the third time and refuses to treat it like noise.

These are the real innovators.
Not idea people. Tension people.
Because they understand something foundational:

You don't need more ideas. You need better senses.

Throughout my career at companies like Qualcomm, Skyworks and Linksys, there were those handful of engineers (I'd say Qualcomm had more than a handful, but for dramatic effect, humor me) who weren't just working on designs.

They weren't anchored to their ideas, their methods or the execution. They were more invested in outcomes.

People outcomes.

They carried a burden themselves. As cliché as it sounds, they felt the need to help create a better world.

These individuals were true innovators, and they possessed the same characteristics:

1. They see with objectivity, feel with empathy, and cut through noise with surgical focus.
2. They wield a cross-domain arsenal of knowledge and skills, with deep roots in their craft and a grab bag of solutioning leverage (a network of people, mentors & mentees).
3. They never stop growing because staying relevant is how they stayed useful.
4. They're obsessive in pursuit, but disciplined in scope; so, they're careful about what they take on.
5. Their ideas are not their babies; they walk away fast when human benefit and relief don't show up.
6. They don't protect solutions, power structures, or egos, they protect users by reorganizing complexity in ways that preserve clarity, expand agency, and reduce future burden for people, even if it means undoing their own work.
7. They know that every benefit they create will eventually be a future source of friction, so they build or plan safeguards, buffers or roadmaps to address them down the line.
8. They deeply sense invisible friction, whether emotional, cognitive, interpersonal, or systemic, typically before the market does.
9. They fearlessly run toward entropy and calamity like firemen into burning buildings, seeing disorder not as chaos, but as the next great invitation to innovate.
10. They're benevolent misfits. Wired to help, and often misunderstood. Because what they see and feel can't always be put to words, but their solutions told the story.

At Apple, there were many like this.
I was fortunate enough to learn and grow because of them.

And if you didn't come in with all these attributes, we helped you grow them, if you were open and willing to let them in.

That was the real job.
Not to defend ideas. Not to perform cleverness.
But to develop instincts.

To notice what others ignored.

To stay uncomfortably curious.
To challenge what felt "fine."
To follow the friction, not for drama, but for direction.

We didn't fall in love with our products.
We fell in love with making them feel smooth and intuitive.
More natural. Less burdensome.

We weren't there to create perfection.
We were there to ease tension.

That's what makes a real innovator.
And that's the real secret sauce.

The Infinite Loop Isn't Just an Address (∞ - CH 2. Principle of Utility as Context Dependent, CH 16)

When I first started at Apple its headquarters was located at 1 Infinite Loop in Cupertino.

Just to clarify, an "Infinite Loop" is a programming term that refers to code that never ends unless it is stopped externally. However, it also reflected Apple's vision of endless innovation.

It's a perfect metaphor for what innovation really is.

It's not just a loop of fixes and flaws. It's a living cycle. Sometimes you have to mine for what's quietly burdening the user. But the real innovator knows that even when nothing's broken, something better will show up… and possibility itself becomes a byproduct.

Here's how it works:
1. A burden is unearthed, noticed, captured
2. A solution is created to address it
3. That solution becomes the new normal
4. New burdens emerge from the solution or its new context
5. The cycle repeats

This is the foundational cycle described in *The Infinite Path*.
And once you understand this law, you stop chasing "finished."
You stop thinking solely in projects.

You start thinking in systems.

You start to realize that what you're building isn't just a product, it's a link in a chain that's been unfolding since before you got here.

And will keep unfolding long after you're gone.

Still skeptical?
Wait 'til Chapter 12.

Why Most Companies Burn Out (and We Didn't)

Many organizations treat innovation like a sprint.
They rally. They plan. They ship.
Then they move on.

But here's the problem:

> The moment you stop moving, the burdens start catching up.

That's why so many promising companies plateau.
They solve an early pain point. They scale. Then they slow.
Meanwhile, burdens pile up, slowly, then suddenly.

And by the time they notice.
It's too late.

Apple didn't fall into this trap because we assumed everything would eventually create its own issues. We didn't view friction as failure. We viewed it as feedback.

So, we'd keep moving. Learning. And unearthing burdens.
Even when things were "good enough."
Especially when they were "good enough."

Because "good enough" is where entropy likes to hide.
And tension detection through a sensitivity to people burdens,
that's how you beat it back down.

Tension Detection as an Operating System

This is the key difference:

Many companies have innovation teams.
The best companies are innovation systems.

That means:
- Everyone is empowered to surface tension.
- Every layer of the org has feedback loops.
- Every decision includes burden forecasting.
- Every process includes escape routes.
- Every improvement is treated as temporary.

At Apple, this meant engineers, designers, operations people;
everyone and anyone (under the platform specific NDA) flagged
product-market issues early, not just after launch.

It meant designers paired up with support teams to observe real
user friction.

It meant individual contributors and leads alike, walked the
factory line.

It meant loads and loads of data on the frictions and aspirations
assured meaningfulness to the user and lower risk for Apple,
simultaneously.

It meant we cared more about removing headaches than adding
features for features-sake.

That's what leads to magic:

A company where every person is a sensor.

The Cycle Never Ends… But That's the Fun Part (∞ - Origins of Innovation, CH 3)

If the Law of Perpetual Innovation feels exhausting, it's only because you've yet to understand that it's inherently a natural part of life. Every single aspect of it.

Innovation isn't a modern idea, it's ancient biology. The word best describes human-driven creations, but before we ever filed patents or held brainstorms, nature had already mastered the playbook.

A genetic mutation eases survival pressure, a burden. A lizard grows sticky feet to grip tree bark, that's Naturally Occurring Utility. But when that adaptation spreads, when the whole species evolves with it? That's Naturally Occurring Innovation. Survival scaled. Evolution. Nature's version of product-market fit.

So when you embrace the cycle, everything changes.

You stop aiming for perfection.
You aim for flow.

You start enjoying the challenge of unearthing the next layer of refinement. You start celebrating smaller wins. You build momentum, not through big bets, but through constant tuning.

Innovation becomes a lifestyle, not a launch.

And that's where the real joy lives.

Not in the keynote.
Not in the press.
But in that quiet moment when something that used to be hard now feels easy.

When a user smiles because you removed a burden they didn't even know they had.
That's the reward.
That's the high.

That's what makes this endless cycle so beautiful. Because it keeps offering you a place to contribute. A place to make things feel just a little more right, for someone, somewhere.

You Already Have the Sauce

People keep looking for some secret playbook. Some template. Some proven roadmap.

But here's the truth:

You may already have everything you need.

You have users.
You have aspiration.
You have frictions.
You have emotions.

And if you're willing to listen, I mean really listen, to that friction…

You'll see the future before it becomes obvious.

You'll ship the thing others only imagined.
You'll build the team others can't replicate.
You'll create flow where others create noise.

And when people ask you what your secret sauce is…

Just smile.
And point to the stove.

Because you know:
It's not vision.
It's not luck.
It's not tech.

It's a deep ability to sense and detect burden and tension, for the sake of restoring relief. Benefit. Agency. That's the real secret sauce.

∞ Reference: The Infinite Path

CHAPTER 11

The Sauce in Action. What Innovating Looks Like.

An Innovation Session – Because Nothing Beats Witnessing the Burden Firsthand

If you want to see what real innovation efforts looks like, not the polished keynote version, but the real, sweaty, productive, borderline-chaotic version, come with me to January 2016.

I flew out to Japan with a team of some of the top minds behind Apple Watch, iPhone, iPad, and SEG Packaging. Our mission? To meet with one of our most trusted component suppliers and co-innovate directly, brutally, and without ceremony.

This wasn't my first rodeo with this model. I'd run sessions like this years prior, before Apple, and it proved exactly how fast burdens could dissolve when builders face each other directly.

The method was familiar. The playground was different. Strip away the layers that typically dilute urgency.

No in-between people. No sanitized decks. No polished demos. Just source and destination. Just the people who build the guts, and the people trying to fit them into the body of a product with micron-level constraints and billion-dollar stakes.

We had one goal:

Push past the current space, energy, and performance limits to unburden future products, so that they could better unburden the customer.

That's what innovation actually is.
Not "cool stuff."
Not feature creep.
Not vision boards.

Just real-time relief.

Burden Transfer: From Supplier to Platform to Person

Inside Apple products, everything is scarce. Space. Height.
Power. Thermal headroom. Durability. Availability. All of it.

And here's the part most people miss: those constraints
compound.
Not linearly.
Exponentially.

Every year.

So we weren't just solving for today's limits. We were solving for
those of tomorrow. Because every feature Apple wanted to ship
in the future, be it health tracking, camera stabilization, faster
charging, and so on, was going to hit a wall unless we started
subtracting the right burdens now.

The logic was simple: the more we could unburden the product,
the more the product could unburden the user. That's it.

Cutting the Noise

To make that happen, we had to cut the noise. So we removed
all the middle layers, the salespeople, application engineers,
component engineers, global supply managers, and anyone
whose job wasn't directly building or integrating the component.

Instead of handoffs and translation layers, we brought the factory
design engineers face-to-face with Apple platform experts. Six
people from each side. No PowerPoints. Just whiteboards,
technical prowess, constraint-sharing, and open minds.

The supplier knew their limitations better than we ever would.
We knew ours better than they ever could.
So we shared our burdens and they shared theirs, no sharing of proprietary content, just collaborative vulnerability.

The result?

Months, possibly years, shaved off our roadmap.
Fewer misunderstandings.
Less churn.
More magic.

They Thought I Was Nuts

Some of my colleagues in leadership thought I was insane.
"There's no way the supplier agrees to this," they told me.

But not everyone saw it that way.

Several higher-up leaders inside Apple immediately got it. They understood that bypassing the middle layers and going supplier-to-customer-direct was not just bold, it was efficient.

As for the supplier's sales team, they were hesitant. They weren't used to this type of collaboration. But when they took it up the chain, something shifted.

Their leadership didn't just agree, they leaned in hard. Because they understood exactly what this was: a chance to skip the theater and go burden-to-burden.

They understood the value of staring friction in the face.

Ultimately, all right decision-makers understood that witnessing pain firsthand and not hearing about it secondhand could be transformative.

Once the greenlight came down from both sides, our teams rallied. And now, everyone was bought in.

That was the bet. And it paid off.

My Ridiculous Rules

Now, if you ask the folks who were there, they'll probably still laugh at some of the rules I set.

- 12 innovators total, 6 from each company
- All windows covered.
- No food. Only water.
- Room set to 70°F.
- A bell. A timer.
- Seven whiteboards.
- No pre-failure without substitution (if you shoot down an idea, you must offer something better). Or you get kicked out!
- One whiteboard listing all 12 innovators and their specialties, for breakout group formation.
- Breakout session leadership rotates across all 12 people.

Sounds nuts? Maybe.
Did it work? Absolutely.

Each person got a turn leading a breakout. They'd bring up a burden, whether technical, systemic, or strategic, and then create breakout teams to help them unpack it. We ran each session on a tight clock, filmed the outcomes, and captured a two-minute summary from each breakout leader.

And yes, we took a photo of every team after each session. Not for PR. For accountability.

We did this for two straight days.

The result?
A tsunami of ideas.

But more importantly: a deep, visceral understanding of each other's constraints. Each other's burdens.

And that's where the real breakthroughs come from.

Make the "Non-Engineers" Part of It

Here's something that matters. I brought global supply managers into the entire session.

- Not to sit on the side.
- To run the bell.
- To keep time.
- To film the sessions.
- To participate.

Why? Because they're the people who ensure we have enough of the components we just co-innovated on to actually build the product. Without them, nothing ships.

Innovation doesn't happen in a silo.

It happens when everyone with a hand in the product, including the logistics and ops people, shares the same emotional context for what's at stake.

They saw the sweat. The tension. The stakes. And they carried that into every negotiation, every forecast, every manufacturing escalation.

From Cynicism to Relentless Creation

At the start, some of the Apple experts rolled their eyes at my setup. I asked them to bring notebooks, to document extra ideas, to keep the creative momentum going between sessions.

They were cynical. At first.

After the session?

They couldn't stop.

They were still drawing, sketching, iterating, on the train, on the plane, in the hotel. I eventually had to sit in a separate train car just to get some rest.

That's the thing about emotional salience.

Once someone lives and feels the burden, the creativity doesn't need to be extracted. It pours out. It's compulsive.

Because innovation is addictive once you've tasted the relief it can create.

Optimizing the Formula

I ran two more of these sessions over the years, often brought in as an internal consultant for confidential, high-stakes initiatives.

Each time, the format got tighter.
The questions got sharper.
The friction got more visible.

Why?

Because we weren't chasing features, instead, we'd listen harder to what people were trying to get free from.

The Core Insight

At the heart of all this is one brutal, freeing truth:

Innovation is not a celebration of creativity. It's a response to burden.

Every product, system, and service exists because something hurt.

Something was too slow.
Too awkward.
Too expensive.
Too complicated.
Too disappointing.
Too painful.

And if your idea doesn't relieve something real?
It doesn't matter how clever it is.

It will die on arrival.

As I wrote in *The Infinite Path*, every act of meaningful utility creation is a reaction to a byproduct, to a burden, to something that someone had to work around, work through or is still having to work with even though better is possible.

When you create without burden, you get theater.
When you create from burden, you get movement.

Rousseau Had It Right (∞ - Principle of Utility as Reactive, CH 16)

Jean-Jacques Rousseau, in his seminal book *The Social Contract* (1762) wrote,

> "Man is born free, and everywhere he is in chains."

That's it.
That's the work.

Every good and service we've ever created from the dawn of civilization is an attempt to break one of those chains.

But here's the catch, and the engine behind *The Law of Perpetual Innovation*:

> Every chain we break spawn's new ones.

The iPhone Camera – How Relief Gets Replaced (∞ - Principle of Perpetual Innovation through Byproduct, CH 13)

You relieve the burden of carrying a separate camera.
Now everyone uses their iPhone to capture life: the kids, sunsets, receipts, everything.

But soon, they want more.
Low-light sucks. Zoom's a joke. Portraits feel flat.

So Apple adds a multi-lens system, night mode, better sensors. Suddenly the phone competes with DSLRs and often wins.

But that new power brings new weight.
Photos eat up storage. File sizes balloon. People lose track of their best shots.

So Apple responds again. On-device machine learning curates your memories, de-duplicates photos, syncs across iCloud, auto-tags the dog, the baby, and the ex you're trying to forget.

Relief. Then weight. Then relief again.

That's not broken design. That's innovation doing its job.
There's no finish line.
Only a loop.

Solve a burden → deliver a benefit → accumulate new burdens → solve again.

That's always been the game.

The Sauce Isn't a Product. It's a Reflex. (∞ - Module D)

You don't need more brainstorms.
You need more burden-sensing.

You need cross-functional sessions where the supplier hears what the designer is panicking about. Where the ops team sees how a packaging constraint delays a board spin. Where everyone shares the same white-hot clarity about what the user is struggling with, or what the system is silently absorbing.

Because that's where the next leap hides.

Not in the pitch deck.
In the pressure.

∞ Reference: The Infinite Path

CHAPTER 12

The Sauce's DNA. From Surviving to Thriving.

How Innovation Always Traces Back to What Makes Us Human (∞ - CH 6 – CH 8)

Remember how in the previous chapter I said this cycle has been going on since the dawn of civilization?

If we zoom out of the iPhone camera example and look at the byproduct–utility loop across time, you'll see the pattern better.

From Cave Dust to Camera Roll

Let's rewind. Before we had iPhones, we had digital cameras.
Before that, film cameras.
Before that, oil paintings.
Before that, drawings on papyrus
Before that, charcoal on cave walls.

And whatever else was in between.

But the goal was the same: to capture what we saw, what we felt, what we didn't want to lose.

Let's call it "Witnessed scene capture" if you will.

Cave paintings weren't art galleries. They were records.
Proof of presence. Markers of memory.
"I was here. We hunted this. We survived that."

Utility delivered? Relief from forgetting. Relief from invisibility.
Burden resolved? Cognitive loss. Legacy loss. Identity loss.

That's innovation.
Messy, primitive, brilliant.

Until it created its own problem.

The cave paintings didn't move. But we had to.
They were stuck inside a cave.

So eventually we made scrolls. Papyrus. Portraits. Frescoes.
Now the memory could travel.

But now you needed a skilled hand.
Painting took time. Cost money. And only few people could do it.
So, you guessed it, we innovated again.

Enter the film camera.
Suddenly anyone could preserve reality. Real people. Real
moments. No charcoal or paint required.

But now you had to wait for film to develop. You crossed your
fingers. You prayed your eyes weren't closed in the one shot you
really wanted.

Next innovation? Digital cameras.
Immediate preview. Unlimited storage. Retake till perfect.

New burden? Image overload. No organization. Emotionally flat.

Then eventually came the iPhone.
Shoot, edit, share. All in your pocket.
Cameras that think for you.
Smart HDR. Night mode. Deep Fusion.

And what happened?

People started comparing their shots to others. Aspirational
tension. A sense that even their best photo could have been
better. The delight was there, sure. But so was the creeping
sense of "not quite."

That's the loop.
Relief → New Burden → New Relief.

From chalk & spit to 48 megapixels.
Still trying to hold on to something we saw, something we felt.

But here's the point:

It was never about the tools.
It was always about the need. The benefits. The utility.

The 19 Human Origin Utilities: Immutable, Eternal, and Alive

In *The Infinite Path*, I introduce a framework and a law that most people never realize they've been living inside of:

The 19 Human Origin Utilities (HOUs)

They're not technologies.
They're not features.
They're not buzzwords.

They are the underlying human needs that all meaningful innovation has been mapping back into since the dawn of civilization. And here's the catch:

Innovation evolves. The Human Origin Utilities do not. So long we remain human, they're constants.

Whether you're solving for transportation, hunger, emotion, or connection, you're always tapping one or more of these 19.

Here are several of them (we're not spilling them all here, they're in *The Infinite Path*):

1. Movement and Locomotion
2. Perception and Sensory Processing
3. Communication and Language
   ...
19. Learning and Knowledge Acquisition

Every human-driven product on the planet, that sticks.
That spreads. That succeeds.

It does so because it relieves a burden tied to at least one of these 19.

The iPhone camera isn't just a lens.
It's a relief machine for Memory and Cognition.
A pressure release valve for the burden of forgetting.

Let's go deeper to show how this plays out.

Witnessed Scene Capture — Where It All Ties Back To (∞ - CH 8, CH 29)

The ability to capture, preserve, and revisit a scene, be it with chalk, shutter, or sensor, doesn't exist in isolation. It was always about the human needs or benefits hiding underneath that tie back to a deeper Human Origin Utility.

Whether it was a hunter tracing bison on limestone, or your kid snapping ten selfies to get the light just right, "Witnessed Scene Capture" ties back to the below five Human Origin Utilities:

1. **Memory and Cognition**: Because we want to remember. To preserve. To offload the burden of forgetting moments that matter, whether they're survival-critical or sentimentally priceless.

2. **Emotional Regulation and Fulfillment**: Because moments carry weight. Joy, loss, pride, nostalgia. They live in images long after they've passed in real life. We capture to relive, to soothe, to anchor our emotional world in something tangible.

3. **Perception and Sensory Processing**: Because some things we see, feel too good, too painful, or too rare to lose. We're not just capturing the image; we're honoring the visual experience.

4. **Artistic Expression and Creativity**: Because we want others to see what we saw, the way we saw it. Not just the pixels, but the feeling. The point of view. The "you had to be there" turned into "you can be."

5. **Communication and Language**: Because sometimes, words aren't enough. A captured scene says what paragraphs can't. It translates presence across time and space, letting us show others exactly what we saw, without the risk of being misheard or misremembered.

These are five of the Human Origin Utilities.
Core needs. The bedrock of why any of this matters.

Cameras don't serve one of these, they serve all five.
That's why they stuck. That's why they keep evolving.

"Witnessed scene capture" was never a gimmick. It's a portal back into what made us feel, think, or matter. And when a new way of capturing scenes shows up, be it cleaner, faster, more expressive, it relieves the burden each of those five utilities was carrying just a little too long.

That's why you adopted it.
Not because it was new.
But because it's human.

It's important to point out, however, that situational context will always determine how "goods and services" tie back into these Human Origin Utilities (HOUs).

For if a camera is being used to capture driver's breaking the law, then that "good" is also tying back to the HOU of *Protection and Shelter*.

And those Human Origin Utilities, they haven't changed.
What has changed is how much personal energy we have to expend fulfilling them.

Be it physical, emotional, cognitive, social or contextual energy:

Innovation has always been about offloading effort, from us to a system, from muscle to mechanism, from person to product.

And now it's time to get visceral. With Cheeseburgers!

Cheeseburgers and the Caloric Savings of Innovation
(∞ - CH 9)

Let's zoom in on a different human origin utility: *Movement and Locomotion*.

What does it take to get from New York to California?

Well… that depends on the century you were born in.

Thousands of years ago?
You'd walk.

That's about 3,300 miles. On foot.
With supplies.

So if you're 165 pounds (75 kg) and carry 44 lbs (20 kg) of gear.
Your daily caloric cost? High.
The journey? Brutal.

Estimated time: 358 days
Estimated energy spent: 1,435,000 food calories
That's roughly 2,870 cheeseburgers at 500 calories each.

You burned your way to your destination.
Literal body mass converted into movement. Cognition. Emotion.
Burdens: High energy cost, danger, shelter needs, constant foraging, fatigue, stress, anger, and on and on.
Not a straight line at all.

So, what did we do?

We innovated.

1. **We rode Horses**
   Relief: Cut the burden. Less walking. More distance.
   New burden: Feed the horse. Care for the horse. Limited terrain. Still slow.

2. **Then we rode Trains & Wagons**
   Relief: Now you can move people and goods across hundreds of miles, faster.
   New burden: Infrastructure dependency. Scheduled travel. Limited freedom of route.
3. **Then we drove Cars**
   Relief: Personalized mobility. Route freedom. Faster speeds.
   New burden: Maintenance. Cost. Accidents. Cognitive load while driving.
4. **And today we ride Airplanes**

Now back to our NY-to-CA traveler.

On a flight, it takes 6 hours and 42 minutes across 2,469 miles from JFK to LAX.
Calories burned while sitting? 503.
Roughly one cheeseburger.

Let that sink in:

From 2,870 cheeseburgers to 1.
From 68,880 hours (358 days) to under 7 hours.

That's what innovation does.
Not just faster.
Not just fancier.

It transfers the energetic burden away from you.
Away from your muscles.
Away from your mind.
Away from your emotional bandwidth.

Away from your social standing.

Because let's be real.
If you walked that distance?

By the time you show up, your shoes are shredded, your face is sunburnt, your stench has its own zip code, and your vibe says "post-apocalyptic bum."

Innovation Is Reallocation (∞ - CH 9, CH 12)

The real function of innovation isn't speed.
It's not features.
It's not delight.

The purpose of Innovation is the reallocation of energy.

The goal has always been to relieve the human system of excessive, repeated, or unnecessary energetic expense.

And that expense isn't just <u>Physical</u>.

It's also:

- <u>Cognitive</u> (mental bandwidth)
- <u>Emotional</u> (stress, guilt, confusion, fear)
- <u>Social</u> (belonging, pressure, status)
- <u>Contextual</u> (misalignment between what the environment demands and what you're equipped to do)

Innovation shows up when one or more of these areas are being over-taxed or taxed without our full conscious awareness.

That's what the Human Origin Utilities track.

They're not abstract categories.
They are mapped to measurable energetic cost.

And all human-driven innovation, EVER, is just a long chain of finding new ways to:

Spend less of your energy.
And shift that burden into a tool, system, service or even another person (unfortunately).

This Is Why "Delight" Happens

That feeling people get when something "just works"?
That's not magic.

That's byproduct burden being lifted, in real-time.

Innovation isn't a surprise party.
It's a subconscious exhale.

"Thank God this flight doesn't take 358 days."
"Thank God this camera made my baby's eyes look perfect."
"Thank God I didn't have to walk to the store. Again."

That's what Apple knows.
That's what great companies and entrepreneurs tap into.
And it's exactly what you should be looking for when you innovate.

Not "what's cool."

But:

Where are people being taxed; silently, subtly, or screaming out loud?

And what will we build that takes that burden away before they even ask?

Final Thought: The Future Is in the 19 (∞ - CH 8, CH 29)

You don't need to memorize the 19 Human Origin Utilities.

You just need to respect that they're always there.

Every product you build, every service you create, every system you design, it either relieves a burden tied to at least one of them, or it doesn't matter.

Or worse, it disrupts them (famine, pollution, crime, etc.).

All great innovation is just less drag on the human experience.
From the cave wall to the camera roll.
From 2,870 cheeseburgers to 1.

From friction… to flight.

That's the sauce.
That's the loop.
That's *The Infinite Path* we're all on.

∞ Reference: The Infinite Path

CONCLUSION

And The Cycle Continues

There's a moment, after every launch, where the applause dies down and the lights go off and all that's left is the system you've built, quietly absorbing the next wave of burden.

If this book has done its job, you now understand that this moment is not the end of innovation.

It's the beginning of the next cycle.

Human-Driven Innovation isn't what happens when you have a good idea. It's what happens when you respond to the frictions that some previously realized solution left behind.

This is the Law of Perpetual Innovation.
And once you see it, you can't unsee it.

What This Book Has Really Been About

The Apple Sauce is not a story about how to build products like Apple. It's a story about how to see, think and feel like Apple. But not just Apple.

Great companies, entrepreneurs and innovators alike.

And more importantly, it's about how to sense like an innovator. Not someone who chases the "next big thing."
But someone who can recognize the next small burden.

Because behind every leap forward, there's usually someone who's carrying burdens that someone like you can remove.

Over the past twelve chapters, we've walked through a simple but profound truth:

Innovation is not born from inspiration. It's born from irritation.

We just gave it a name: burden.
Within *The Infinite Path,* we call it Byproduct.
And to manage that burden, there's a framework:

The Law of Perpetual Innovation

The concepts shared here, if you've followed the ∞ symbols throughout this book, are references to deeper ideas that come from my more comprehensive book: *The Infinite Path*.

You've been reading distilled, practical applications of these deeper theories and principles born from the real trenches of product teams, escalations, late-night reviews, and quiet breakthroughs over the past 29 years.

What You've Had All Along

If some part of this book felt familiar, good. That's not a coincidence.

Because the ability to think this way? You already have it.

You've felt the friction. You've noticed what doesn't feel right. You've seen people struggle with things that could be smoother, easier, more intuitive. Maybe you just didn't have the structure to act on it. Or the language to defend it.

That's what this book aimed to give you. Not just clarity, but confidence.

Confidence to see irritation as insight. To treat constraints like signals. To organize the instinct you already have in a way that drives real outcomes:

Better products.
Stronger leadership.
And more trust with the people you serve.

Because that's what innovation actually is.

It's not about being clever.
It's about being useful.

And the most useful thing you can be is someone who lifts the weight off others.
Systematically.
Repeatedly.
Elegantly.

You don't have to build the next iPhone.

But you can become the kind of person who builds like the people who did.

And if this book helped you take even one step closer to that?

Then the work is already working.

∞ See you on the path.

FURTHER READING

The Infinite Path – The Law of Perpetual Innovation

If *The Apple Sauce* stirred something in you, an intuition, a question, a desire to go deeper, then you may be ready for:

The Infinite Path – The Law of Perpetual Innovation

The Apple Sauce was never meant to be the whole recipe. It's the first taste. The distilled notes from a longer conversation.

Where *The Apple Sauce* gives you the instincts, *The Infinite Path* gives you the entire operating system.

I wrote *The Apple Sauce* because I knew *The Infinite Path* would feel like a lot for most readers. Not for the academics. Not for the hardcore systems thinkers or innovation junkies. They'll love it.

But for everyone else?

It's a 550-page heavyweight. Part reference manual, part philosophical deep-dive, part textbook; loaded with concepts, principles, and math formula's you've never seen before. Like:

- The Byproduct-Utility Disruption Function
- The Innovation Driver Function (aka The Innovation Equation)
- The Byproduct Emergence Function
- The Utility Abandonment Condition (aka The Byproduct Tolerance Threshold)
And more…

In *The Infinite Path*, you'll see innovation not as invention but as thermodynamic inevitability.

Entropy isn't just a physics buzzword. It's the invisible force degrading every product, service, and system ever experienced.

It wears things down. Not just physically, but psychologically. As things degrade, so does a user's sense of benefit.

- 65 Absolute types of Utility
- 34 Byproduct taxonomy types
- 19 Human Origin Utilities
- 15 Intensities of how Subjective Byproduct may be perceived
- 14 Indicators of Objective Byproduct severity
- 6 Innovation Methods (through LPI's byproduct-utility lens)
    - Incremental Sustained Innovation
    - Innovation through Utility Integration
    - Innovation through Utility Specialization
    - Adaptive Utility Innovation
    - Modular Utility Innovation
    - Radical Innovation
- 2 new Theorems (Byproduct Emergence & Constant Utility)
    - The Byproduct Emergence Theorem
    - The Theory of Constant Utility
- 1 new Law
    - The Law of Conservation of Human Utility

∞ Explore it when you're ready.

https://the-infinite-path.com

BIBLIOGRAPHY

Martinez, P. A. (2025), *The Infinite Path: The Law of Perpetual Innovation.* Franklin Publishers.

Impact Models

- **A complete taxonomy of 34 byproduct classes**: spanning emotional, functional, social, environmental, systemic, aesthetic, and ethical categories.
- **An exhaustive list of 65 Absolute Utility types**: that cover every reason people choose products, services, and systems.
- **The Impact Spectrum and Byproduct Contrast Continuum**: Frameworks to aid classifying, scoring, and prioritizing which burdens to solve based on scale, emotional salience, and systemic risk, for the inseparable objective and subjective dimensions of byproduct.

Utility Pursuit

- **Byproduct-Driven Utility Pursuit**: A reframed understanding of why humans actually pursue utility.
- **The concept of Forescension**: The moment a person decides, emotionally and cognitively, that their current burden is no longer acceptable, and leaps toward something perceived as better.
- **AI based Byproduct Driven Innovation (AI-BDIE)**: How an organization can develop a true AI product-development engine that can yield a high probability of market success, and why.

Innovation Methods

- **6 Innovation Methods**: Through the lens of LPI's byproduct-utility causality loop you'll learn how to maximize the use of:
  - Incremental Sustained Innovation
  - Innovation through Utility Integration
  - Innovation through Utility Specialization
  - Adaptive Utility Innovation
  - Modular Utility Innovation
  - Radical Innovation

An Itemized List of what's in *The Infinite Path*:

- 108 Principles on Utility and Byproduct
  - The Cardinal Principle of Byproduct Emergence from Experienced and Potential Utility
  - 56 Byproduct Principles
  - 50+1 Utility Principles